D1006369

DEVELOPING UNIVERSITY-INDUSTRY RELATIONS

Pathways to Innovation from the West Coast

Robert C. Miller,

Bernard J. Le Boeuf,

and Associates

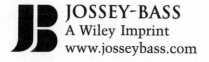

JOSSEY-BASS
A Wiley Imprint
www.josseybass.com

Copyright © 2009 by John Wiley & Sons, Inc. All rights reserved.

Published by Jossey-Bass
A Wiley Imprint
989 Market Street, San Francisco, CA 94103-1741—www.josseybass.com

No part of this publication may be reproduced, stored in a retrieval system, or transmitted in any form or by any means, electronic, mechanical, photocopying, recording, scanning, or otherwise, except as permitted under Section 107 or 108 of the 1976 United States Copyright Act, without either the prior written permission of the publisher, or authorization through payment of the appropriate per-copy fee to the Copyright Clearance Center, Inc., 222 Rosewood Drive, Danvers, MA 01923, 978-750-8400, fax 978-646-8600, or on the Web at www.copyright.com. Requests to the publisher for permission should be addressed to the Permissions Department, John Wiley & Sons, Inc., 111 River Street, Hoboken, NJ 07030, 201-748-6011, fax 201-748-6008, or online at www.wiley.com/go/permissions.

Readers should be aware that Internet Web sites offered as citations and/or sources for further information may have changed or disappeared between the time this was written and when it is read.

Limit of Liability/Disclaimer of Warranty: While the publisher and author have used their best efforts in preparing this book, they make no representations or warranties with respect to the accuracy or completeness of the contents of this book and specifically disclaim any implied warranties of merchantability or fitness for a particular purpose. No warranty may be created or extended by sales representatives or written sales materials. The advice and strategies contained herein may not be suitable for your situation. You should consult with a professional where appropriate. Neither the publisher nor author shall be liable for any loss of profit or any other commercial damages, including but not limited to special, incidental, consequential, or other damages.

Jossey-Bass books and products are available through most bookstores. To contact Jossey-Bass directly call our Customer Care Department within the U.S. at 800-956-7739, outside the U.S. at 317-572-3986, or fax 317-572-4002.

Jossey-Bass also publishes its books in a variety of electronic formats. Some content that appears in print may not be available in electronic books.

Library of Congress Cataloging-in-Publication Data

Developing university-industry realtions : pathways to innovation from the West Coast / [edited by] Robert C. Miller, Bernard Le Boeuf, and associates, – 1st ed.
   p. cm.
   Includes bibliographical references and index.
   ISBN 978-0-470-43396-6 (cloth)
   1. Business and education–Pacific States. 2. Business and education–British Columbia. 3. Technology transfer–Pacific States. 4. Technology transfer–British Columbia. I. Miller, Robert C., 1942-II. Le Boeuf, Bernard, 1934-
   LC1085.3.P165D48 2009
   371.19'5–dc22
                       2008055668

Printed in the United States of America

FIRST EDITION
HB Printing 10 9 8 7 6 5 4 3 2 1

Contents

PREFACE

Senior leaders in both universities and companies rarely have the time or expertise to master the details necessary to manage operations essential for effective university-industry affairs. Yet increasingly, a knowledge-based economy draws universities and companies into close contact and provides significant mutual benefits for university-industry relations. This book shows that there is a path forward. Successful technology transfer helps alleviate such problems for university administrators as (a) diminished political support at the state level for research, (b) faculty criticism of resources going to the technology transfer office, and (c) demands from the public for not being competitive. Familiarity with technology transfer helps the senior administrator see and deal with opportunities.

This book provides a view of university-industry affairs as seen from representatives of some of the most renowned research universities in the world. These campuses are also leading innovators in the development of offices, programs, and institutional mechanisms of technology transfer, licensing, commercialization, and company incubation. The universities—all located on the west coast of North America—have tangible records as invaluable resources for the growth of their regional economies through innovative technology transfer and commercialization initiatives. The point of view reflected in this book is that it is possible to have enormous intellectual integrity and high-quality research simultaneous with being a valuable impetus to regional economic development. This book provides a variety of tested methods, productive demonstrations, and go-to strategies of potential relevance to research universities in general in the United States and around the world.

Our goal is to demonstrate exemplary practices in the full range of technology transfer activities for senior administrators and faculty of universities and business managers in companies. It is written to enable administrators, faculty, and senior management to better understand the new complex world of university-industry affairs by faculty and professionals who make the system work. The book is empirically grounded in examples from which fundamental principles are derived. This book is not intended to serve as a practitioner's how-to guide on the mechanics of technology transfer.

The true value of university-industry collaborations depends on strong university-industry relations. Michael Porter's well-documented studies of the cluster phenomenon of economic growth and competitiveness have heightened awareness of the importance of university-industry relations and the value of university research and innovation in economic development. The challenges, however, are significant and even daunting. Few of the highest-level academic leaders have experience in university-industry relations or in technology transfer. Few senior company executives have participated directly in management of the most relevant operations of university-industry relations, hence relations are constantly at risk for sheer lack of understanding. All too often, operations on the university side are left entirely in the hands of nonacademics and operations in companies can be driven more by lawyers than other relevant professionals. Consequently, relationship-building falls by the wayside—the victim of perceived short-term financial gain or conservative risk management on the university side and by low-cost access and legal protection on the company side.

This book provides examples of effective practices that can form the basis for good university-industry relationships. It demonstrates how university professionals and academics can work together with enlightened company management to establish and maintain good working relations. The chapters are intentionally brief, but detailed enough to document success as experienced by the authors, who emphasize the general principles and procedures that form the basis of their success.

The aim is to describe a set of operations in the university that form the framework for university-industry relations. Each operation has a major impact on the university's ability to manage university-industry affairs, technology deployment, and knowledge transfer to the private sector. The chapters are written by administrators who were keys to the successful operation of their respective offices.

The chapters reflect those offices and organizations that present services to and sign agreements with companies on behalf of universities. Their operations significantly influence how the university is viewed by companies—whether bureaucratic or efficient, entrepreneurial or cautious, timely or slow to respond, protective or facilitative, expert or naive. Views on these matters can then be translated into support for philanthropy and into support in the community and in the political arena. Successful collaborative research has often led to positive lobbying on behalf of university initiatives.

Following an introductory chapter on the context in which university-industry relations occur and the general rules of the game, Robert Miller addresses industry-sponsored research agreements in Chapter 2. These agreements are the most frequently encountered agreements by faculty, students, universities, and companies. On the one hand, they establish positive relationships, train students for the workforce, support faculty research, generate indirect cost funds for infrastructure renewal, and deliver cutting-edge research to the sponsor. On the other hand, contentious negotiations over intellectual property issues or failed deliverables can be detrimental to university-company relations.

In Chapter 3, Katharine Ku presents extensive data on licensing revenue and the philosophy of Stanford toward negotiating licenses. It is widely recognized that Katharine is one of the most experienced directors and manages one of the two or three most successful technology transfer offices in the world. Her analysis presents a clear picture of the financial challenges faced by technology transfer offices and documents the probabilities of success and failure. These data are sobering and should set more realistic expectations and policies for many universities.

In Chapter 4 Charles Williams and Gerald Barnett describe in some detail the approaches to software copyright licensing that Gerald pioneered at the University of Washington in Seattle. The concepts and processes that Gerald and his group developed are distinct from those traditionally used in the standard practice of exclusive licensing of patents. The approach has been particularly successful with the information technology industry, but is generalized to address a wide range of rights to various technologies other than software.

Pat Jones describes the operation of university-industry consortia in Chapter 5, drawing on his experience with the Center for Process Analytical Chemistry (CPAC). This is an NSF-sponsored research center that evolved into a self-supporting center that includes dozens of companies, many from the Fortune 500. Jones describes the nature of this consortium and the policies and procedures that made it so successful. Industry-sponsored consortia are particularly valuable because they support a broad set of faculty, students, and companies with a built-in technology deployment strategy. They also provide for facile and effective knowledge transfer.

In Chapter 6, Angus Livingstone describes the one-stop shopping approach of an integrated office that sees its role broadly as industry liaison. This office has reported for decades to a succession of knowledgeable vice presidents for research at the University of British Columbia, all of whom were intimately involved in university-industry affairs for years as professors. The success of the University of British Columbia University-Industry Liaison Office (UILO) reflects the continuing commitment of both government and the university to this vital function as well as to the dedication of a long-serving set of professionals in the office. The chapter documents the arrangements that made this office so valuable to a province that depended exclusively on revenues from the resource industries of forestry, fishing, and mining before it became a high-tech center for Canada.

In Chapter 7, Ken Walters documents the development and circumstances of start-up companies arising from proactive entrepreneurial research collaborations with the University of Washington. Drawing on rich data from his multiyear study of these companies, Ken summarizes the steps that universities should take to make a positive impact on this important and highly visible element of a vibrant economy.

Mark Betteridge presents the factors in Chapter 8 that led to the success of Discovery Parks Inc. (DPI), a company that manages a set of university-affiliated research parks. DPI has built multitenant facilities on campuses that house start-up companies from the host universities. They also house other small companies seeking research collaboration with the university. In 2002, DPI won the award for the best university-affiliated research park in North America. Mark was the director responsible for this success. It is important to note that DPI was owned and developed by a nonprofit foundation. The boards of directors of both DPI and the foundation had representatives from the universities involved. Eight of the last ten winners of this prestigious award from the Association of University Research Parks (AURP) operate within a similar legal framework—that is, they are not managed by a university.

In Chapter 9, Mary Walshok describes the evolution, processes, and accomplishments of UCSD CONNECT, the premier example of an organization designed to link the university and the business community on a wide variety of fronts. UCSD CONNECT is widely credited with being a key factor in the transformation of San Diego from a city dependent on military budgets to one with a diverse high-tech economy linked to the University of California at San Diego. UCSD CONNECT is the model emulated as a most important element in university efforts to promote economic development. Mary Walshok is the dean who developed and managed UCSD CONNECT and has published widely on the role of universities in innovation and economic development.

We are grateful to Lesa Mitchell, Wayne Johnson, and Mark Betteridge for their support in the many things involved in bringing this manuscript to completion and we thank their organizations, the Kauffman Foundation, Hewlett-Packard, and Discovery Parks, respectively, for funding workshops, travel, and publication costs necessary in this enterprise.

CONTRIBUTORS

Gerald Barnett is director of the Research Technology Enterprise Initiative at the University of Washington. From 2002 to 2008, he was director of the Office for Management of Intellectual Property at the University of California at Santa Cruz. From 1991 to 2002, he led the University of Washington's intellectual property program focused on software and digital media, now called Digital Ventures. He has served on the faculty of the Association of University Technology Managers Software and Digital Media Licensing course since its inception. He received his PhD in English literature from the University of Washington.

Mark Betteridge is president of Mark Betteridge & Associates (MBA) Inc., executive director and CEO of Discovery Parks Trust, vice chair of the Vancouver Economic Development Commission, chair of Covenant House Vancouver, and a founding director of the Greater Vancouver Economic Commission. He is an angel investor in early-stage technology firms. He has held various positions in both private real estate development companies and in municipal management. He was the first president of the University of British Columbia Real Estate Corporation. He received his primary and high school education in England and the United States and holds a BSc (Hons) from Trent University and a Masters degree from the University of Waterloo, in Ontario, Canada.

Patrick D. Jones directs the Office of Technology Transfer at the University of Arizona, and he is the past president for the Association of University Technology Managers (AUTM), a thirty-five-hundred-member professional society supporting professional development and outreach for academic technology transfer. In the public sector, he has held regular and affiliate faculty appointments in chemistry and for six years served in technology transfer at the University of Washington, including in a joint appointment in his final year as assistant dean for University-Industry Affairs in the College of Engineering. At Washington, he participated in the Center for Process Analytical Chemistry as a researcher, interim center administrative director and technology manager responsible for its intellectual property management. His private sector activities have included R&D, product life cycle management, and product marketing. He was the director of product strategy for an Internet managed service provider, the international marketing manager for a small commercial manufacturer of solid-state laser and nonlinear optical systems, as well as a principal research scientist conducting contract research and prototype development in that same firm. He holds a PhD in chemical physics and an MA in business administration.

Katharine Ku is director of the Office of Technology Licensing (OTL) at Stanford University. OTL is responsible for the licensing of various state-of-the-art university technologies and industry-sponsored research agreements and collaborations. From 1994 to 1998, in addition to her OTL responsibilities, Ku was responsible for Stanford's pre-award Sponsored Projects Office. Ku was vice president of business development at Protein Design Labs, Inc. in Mountain View, California from 1990 to 1991. Prior to PDL, she spent twelve years at Stanford in various positions, was a researcher at Monsanto and Sigma Chemical, administered a dialysis clinical trial at University of California, and taught chemistry and basic engineering courses. Ku has been active in the Licensing Executive Society (LES), serving as vice president, western region and trustee of LES and various committee chairs. She served as president of the Association of University Technology Managers (AUTM) from 1988 to 1990. She received the 2001 AUTM Bayh-Dole Award for her efforts in university licensing. Ku has a BS in chemical engineering (Cornell University), an MS in chemical engineering (Washington University in St. Louis), and is a registered patent agent.

Bernard J. Le Boeuf has been vice chancellor for research or associate vice chancellor for research at the University of California at Santa Cruz since 1999 and directs the Aligned

Research Program of the University Affiliated Research Center at NASA Ames. He received his BA and PhD from the University of California at Berkeley. He has been a professor and research professor of biology at the University of California at Santa Cruz since 1968, publishing over 160 research articles and three books on marine mammal behavior and physiology. He stopped teaching in 1994, did consulting work with industry for three years, and then returned to the university as an administrator in the Office for Research.

Angus Livingstone is managing director of the University-Industry Liaison Office (UILO) at the University of British Columbia (UBC) and is president of the university's wholly owned subsidiary, UBC Research Enterprises Inc. He graduated from UBC with a BSc in Computer Science in 1983. In 1988, he joined UILO where he has held various positions relating to industry-sponsored research and technology transfer. In 1999, he became the managing director of UILO. Angus is cofounder and president of the Alliance for the Commercialization of Canadian Technology.

Robert C. Miller has had a long, distinguished career as a microbiologist, being a fellow of the Royal Society of Canada, co-recipient of the Gold Medal for Natural Sciences from the Science Council of British Columbia, holder of five U.S. patents, and recipient of numerous honors for research, teaching, and service. He has extensive experience as a university administrator, having served as dean of the Faculty of Science at the University of British Columbia from 1988 to 1995, director and associate vice provost for research and vice provost for intellectual property and technology transfer at the University of Washington from 1995 to 2000, and vice chancellor for research at the University of California at Santa Cruz from 2000 to 2006. Miller received his BS in physics from Trinity College in Hartford, Connecticut, his MS in biophysics from Pennsylvania State University, and his PhD in molecular biology from the University of Pennsylvania.

Kenneth D. Walters has studied university-based start-up companies for the past ten years, particularly those spawned from research at the University of Washington. He has published numerous articles in the Harvard Business Review, California Management Review, and other leading academic journals, and is the author of two books, *Entrepreneurial Management: New Technologies and New Market Development* (Ballinger), and *Nationalized Companies* (McGraw-Hill). For many years a business school dean, Walters received his JD from Stanford Law School and his PhD from the Haas School of Business, University of California at Berkeley. He may be contacted at kwalters@u.washington.edu.

Mary Lindenstein Walshok is associate vice chancellor for Public Programs at the University of California at San Diego (UCSD), Dean of the University Extension, and adjunct professor of sociology. She received her BA from Pomona College and her MA and PhD in sociology from Indiana University. She has been a visiting professor at Stockholm School of Economics for several years and in 2004 held an International Appointment in the Department of Continuing Education, Oxford University, Oxford, England. Walshok is responsible for UCSD's outreach activities including regionally focused programs such as Executive Education, continuing professional education, UCSD-TV and a variety of community and economic development initiatives, including Global CONNECT and the San Diego Dialogue. She is responsible for a staff of 275 and annual revenues of over $30 million. She has authored two books, *Blue Collar Women* and *Knowledge Without Boundaries* (dealing with the role of research universities in the economy), over fifty published articles and book chapters, and a variety of reports on the "new economy" and research capabilities for local and state agencies. She is the recipient of numerous awards including the distinguished Kellogg Foundation's Leadership Fellowship, and Sweden's Royal Order of the Polar Star. Walshok chaired the board of the $400 million San Diego Community Foundation during 2002–2004, and is currently the chair of the board of the International Community Foundation, and serves on the boards of the La Jolla Playhouse, the San Diego Public Library Foundation, and the Girard Foundation.

Charles R. Williams is associate director of the Office of Technology Transfer at the University of Oregon. His work at the University of Oregon focuses on informatics licensing and start-up formation, and he teaches innovation management at the School of Law in a program designed to integrate with the university's technology entrepreneurship program. In 1997, he was one of the first members to join the software and informatics licensing unit formed by Gerald Barnett at the University of Washington, and he is currently program chair for the AUTM Software Course. He was director of the University of Washington TechTransfer Digital Ventures from 2002 to 2007. He has practiced environmental law on behalf of citizens and nonprofit organizations and also represented athletes, artists, and nonprofits in the sports and entertainment industry. He holds a PhD in botany and a JD from the University of Washington.

The Jossey-Bass
Higher and Adult Education Series

CHAPTER ONE

CONTEXT AND CONSTRAINTS

Robert C. Miller and
Bernard J. Le Boeuf

This book is about the transfer of new discoveries and innovation from research conducted at universities to the commercial sector. University-industry relations are the processes between the participants that permit, facilitate, and streamline technology transfer or that make it difficult and cumbersome, as the case may be. The relations involve working out the agreements, licenses, contracts, and conditions for use of the intellectual property that is vital in the path from idea to application.

BAYH-DOLE AND UNIVERSITY-INDUSTRY RELATIONS

Universities are the principal source of inventions and innovation because this is where most fundamental research takes place. Moreover, because most of this research is federally funded, it follows that restrictions by the government on the research it funds can impede technology transfer. This was the situation before 1980. The federal government owned intellectual property rights on research that it funded but too few patents and inventions found their way into commercial use. Congress dealt with this impasse with a critical piece of legislation in 1980, the Bayh-Dole Act, which gave universities ownership of inventions developed through the use of federal funds for research and created strong incentives for technology transfer. By encouraging

1

universities to collaborate with industry on promoting commercialization of inventions, the legislation quickly accelerated the transfer of research to applications by industry. Just ten years after the act was passed, patents to universities had increased six times over their level in the decade before Bayh-Dole. Owing in large part to the Bayh-Dole Act, university research can have a significant impact on local and national economies through university-industry relations.

Nevertheless, there remain problems that universities and industry must deal with such as patent disputes, hostile encounters between public and private ventures, new problems relating to conflict of interest, licensing policy, and royalty distribution. Some question the propriety of commercial relationships for faculty members and university administrators and there is concern over "corporatization" of science. These critics are usually key people who express their concern in newspapers and meetings about commercial interests and conflicts of interest regarding university-industry affairs.

In today's knowledge-based economy, universities augment their primary mission of creating and disseminating knowledge through research and teaching by working with the for-profit sector. Universities do this by engaging in collaborative research with companies; exchanging personnel, materials, and equipment; and by licensing patented university inventions to industry for commercialization. Universities and faculty constantly accept biomaterials, industry-sponsored research materials, collaborative agreements, nondisclosure agreements, and confidential information. Modern research cannot and does not proceed without transfer of materials or contractual agreements. Faculty, universities, and companies do not exchange valuable materials and information without conditions in agreements that are vitally important for efficient exchange. Ironing out these conditional agreements requires university policies governing scientific integrity, conflict of interest, and intellectual property. Intellectual property (IP) management in universities must be given high priority because it can be a sticking point in technology transfer activities and in the university-industry relation enterprise. IP clauses are often contentious because universities seek open disclosure, discourse, and freedom of deployment regarding research results; companies seek as much confidentiality and control as possible. As a result, the intellectual property terms in a contract are difficult to negotiate.

THE CHANGING DYNAMICS OF UNIVERSITY-INDUSTRY RELATIONS

University-industry relations are becoming ever more important as a knowledge-based economy expands. The imperative toward more productive relations between university and industry is driven by the following factors.

Tens of billions of dollars of government-funded research are premised on the value of innovation and basic research in U.S. and Canadian universities. Government recognizes the imperative of a close linkage between universities and the private sector. The university's research mission—to conduct basic research, train new scholars, and create new knowledge—is clearly vital to the government's interest in having companies remain innovative by converting knowledge into useful products and services. In short, the government has ample reason to insist on good university-industry relations.

In recent decades regional economies have increasingly been strengthened by start-up companies derived from university-based discoveries. Fueled by knowledgeable venture capital, start-ups have developed sophisticated systems of assessing early-stage technologies, investment in areas of promise, research and development, new venture mechanics and management, and marketing and sales. These companies not only commercialize products and services from university-based discoveries but provide high-paying jobs for some of the most talented and entrepreneurial university graduates. They also support interesting research in the university.

Many industry-managed research operations have closed or scaled back significantly. Companies now depend more on universities to provide fundamental research results to generate new products and services for an increasingly competitive and innovation-driven market place.

Industry demands graduates that are knowledgeable about research and product development. University-industry cooperative agreements form a sound basis for interesting projects that better prepare graduate students for careers in an industrial environment and supply a stream of new employees to the companies.

At present, universities seek and receive considerable financial support from companies. It is critical, therefore, for universities to bring coherence to the management of all forms of company support and for companies to understand the context and limitations of university contributions to their business operations.

Two Cultures

In reality, good relations between universities and companies are continuously strained by the differences between the cultures that dominate the two entities. Often an agreement cannot be consummated either because the university will not incur risk or the company will lose control. These showstoppers derive from the intrinsic differences associated with each culture, as we shall argue. It is vital, therefore, that each party be aware and sensitive to the culture that controls and governs the other.

University culture derives from its mission of teaching, research, and service and is based on the free exchange of ideas and providing the public with access to an impartial source of information. Each of the three components of the mission is viewed broadly. Education embraces undergraduates, graduate students, extension, and outreach into the community and into the professions. This emphasis makes students' interests paramount. The emphasis in the research arena is on fundamental investigation of issues both basic and applied. Academic freedom allows the university researcher to pursue research agendas with open-ended goals, interact with colleagues, and freely publish the results. Professional schools, such as medicine, conduct a full spectrum of research ranging from basic science to technology development and clinical care. Rarely, however, do universities place a priority on product development including the successive stages of technology or product refinement. Faculty progress and reputation are based on publication of fundamental work in prestigious journals administered by peer review. Pushing the frontiers of knowledge is the ultimate objective and motivator.

The focus of industry, however, places a high value on earnings, profit, return on investment, product or service development, and market growth. Companies are concerned with quarterly results that necessitate short-term goals whereas universities have long-term goals consistent with enhancing the reputations that they have established and measured over decades.

Companies build their brands by depending on a wide range of intellectual property protections, including patents, trade secrets, and copyright protections. In contrast, universities traditionally value open communication, sharing of information with colleagues, and rapid publication of new findings.

Company management is based on hierarchical control with a CEO and a set of officers and managers reporting to top management, which in turn reports to a board of directors. Universities are managed in a system of joint governance wherein responsibility for policy and programs is controlled by a complex set of interactions between a board of regents, governors, or trustees, the university's administrators, and a faculty senate. University governance is typically collegial and consultative, with the president appointed as a senior academic who is not viewed as a company CEO by the faculty. Advancement in the two cultures is managed differently. In a company one's career is influenced heavily by senior management. In the universities it is controlled by colleagues. When senior administrators such as deans complete their administrative service, they usually return to the ranks of faculty.

Policies governing teaching and research are designed to protect the cultural values of the university. These policies are established in the context of the faculty senate, a body that represents the richly diverse set of schools and colleges that make up the university. This means that a complex set of values, objectives, and metrics are debated and evaluated on a continuing basis by university regents, administrators, faculty, students, and staff. It demands operation of a vibrant, contentious political process, because governance involves exercise of political power as well as authority. Vote, influence, and control of financial resources matter. Except for specific organized religions, universities are the longest-standing human institutions. Thus, neither is the university system likely to change dramatically, nor should it.

We emphasize that the university's system of governance affects university policies which in turn affect industry agreements. Different academic disciplines can have quite divergent views on the value of various terms such as intellectual property and other deliverables. Clinicians, for example, rarely encounter IP issues during the course of their research. Computer scientists are usually disinclined to think in terms of patenting software. Pulp and paper engineers frequently want a wide deployment of their technology, and therefore do not wish their patents to be licensed to one exclusive licensee. Conversely, pharmaceutical biochemists are keen to develop a blockbuster drug with an exclusive license to maximize its value. Consequently, university policies as determined by a governance system must reflect the differing perspectives on rights and deliverables that are found in a diverse research community.

Different industries can have remarkably disparate views on IP rights developed from university research. By and large, company expectations follow those of the university research disciplines that support particular industries. On the one hand, with the exception of start-up companies, information technology companies want nonexclusive rights to university-developed technologies at low cost. So do manufacturing, agriculture, and other resource industries. Large pharmaceutical companies ("Big Pharma"), on the other hand, usually demand exclusive rights to the research results supported by them.

To sum up, universities and companies operate in two distinct cultures and systems of management, and different industries and academic disciplines have varying needs. The terms "university" and "industry" are overly simplistic. It is inevitable that joining these two cultures creates challenges for the industry and university collaborators, especially in several key areas: rights to intellectual property, confidentiality versus publication, conflict-of-interest issues, and protection of the public interest. The Council on Government Relations addresses these issues in reports posted on their Web site (www.cogr.edu). Negotiations and relationships need to reflect these differences and IP policies must be tailored to these idiosyncrasies.

CHAPTER TWO

UNIVERSITY-INDUSTRY RESEARCH AGREEMENTS

Robert C. Miller

Industry-sponsored research agreements with universities come in many forms, but there are key elements common to all of them. The agreements are initiated through faculty contacts with companies and are designed to convey research findings and intellectual property rights to the sponsor. They establish a working relationship between the company, the faculty, and the university. They provide a way to share information as well as a training environment for students desiring exposure to industry before graduation and employment. The negotiations, subsequent conduct of the research, and the reporting arrangements can be contentious. The requirements of the agreements and the management of university-company relations demand thoughtful and knowledgeable administration by the university. Initial agreements between a faculty member and a company usually constrain future agreements to one extent or another.

Many factors determine the success of industry-sponsored research agreements. These include timely negotiations, truly best efforts in the conduct of research, meeting timetables on deliverables, graduation of well-trained students who become employees, and results that aid the company and generate first-rate publications. Successful industry-sponsored research agreements establish mutually beneficial relationships between companies and the university.

Positive relationships lead to enhanced training of graduate students, continued support of research, networking opportunities in the industry, advocacy in the public arena, contribution of company employees as adjunct faculty, and philanthropic donations. The dean of Graduate Studies and Research at Stanford University stated that the overall contributions of Hewlett-Packard to the university over the years have greatly outweighed any possible licensing revenues. It is critical, therefore, to understand the circumstances that generally apply in industry-sponsored research and to work toward maximum success.

Relationships

The first order relationship is usually established between a faculty member, who is also the principal investigator (PI), and a senior research manager in a company. If the research benefits both of them, a relationship may develop and expand. Sometimes large projects can be established at the level of the PI interacting with the VP of research or the CEO of the company. University representatives must embrace the opportunity and work hard to shape it into a workable agreement that meets the objectives of the company and the PI on the one hand, and the obligations of the university on the other. Excessive concern that university interests could be compromised by the faculty in orchestrating an agreement thwarts initiation of these relations. Even the largest of our universities have minimal staff to support these relationships. Hundreds of faculty, however, interact with company personnel in many venues, such as international conferences. Consequently, faculty are vitally important as the primary marketers of their research and they are the first point of contact with industry liaisons.

Faculty are responsible for the deliverables embedded in the agreement and therefore are ultimately responsible for the conduct of a university-industry research project. Therefore, it is critical that faculty understand the exact nature of university policies and procedures governing the terms of the agreements and the expectations of the company. The terms of deliverables are controversial within the university community. On the one hand, many tolerate only an annual report as the deliverable, given that the university policy is to conduct fundamental research; quarterly reports to the company are thus seen as an unusual burden for faculty. On the other hand, many universities agree to specific work plans with periodic meetings to review progress with the sponsor. Several universities even agree to develop prototypes of inventions and provide funds or manage grants to facilitate prototype development. Some universities agree to "best efforts" on deliverables and others agree only to "reasonable efforts." Whatever the deliverables and whatever the term of effort agreed upon, it is critical that the faculty be informed and that they agree to the terms of any particular agreement.

The university has much to gain from positive relationships established in university-industry projects. First, positive relationships lead to enhanced training of graduate students as they work between faculty and company researchers. This develops experience in meeting objectives and milestones that are of vital importance in the commercial world, while at the same time pursuing research in the collegial environment of the university. This experience is not found in other venues. The graduates frequently find employment with their sponsors. Relevant experience leads to higher starting salaries for students who have interned in work related to university-industry agreements. For example, MBA students at the University of Washington who worked with licensing officers started at $10,000 higher than their counterparts because of their acquired knowledge in structuring and negotiating deals.

Second, the relationship can lead to continued or expanded projects and can include advocacy for larger research programs such as those sponsored by consortia. A reputation as a poor partner can thwart the university's ability to attract significant projects.

Third, successful projects can lead to advocacy in a wider realm, such as the state legislature. A good example comes from the relationship between Dr. Bruce Montgomery (vice president of Pathogenesis), the Cystic Fibrosis Foundation, and Dr. Maynard Olson (professor at the University of Washington). The University of Washington entered into an agreement to sequence the genome of *Pseudomonas aeriginosa*, the opportunistic pathogen that causes extensive damage to cystic fibrosis patients. Within a relatively short time an appropriate research agreement was concluded among the participants with the company,

Pathogenesis, and the Cystic Fibrosis Foundation, the sponsors. Dr. Olson's group made rapid progress, and Pathogenesis successfully exploited the information derived from the project. Subsequently, the University of Washington approached the legislature with an innovative proposal for clusters of faculty positions designed to have an impact in specific research areas. Dr. Montgomery gave testimony in the legislature to the value of such clusters and addressed specifically the outstanding work done by Olson's group and the critical role played by the University of Washington. This and similar testimony from other companies led to a unanimous, positive vote in committees of the Senate and House that led to passage of the bill and a significant number of new faculty for the university. Given that these were tenured positions, the bill dedicated permanent funds equivalent to a large endowment. Few licensed technologies have generated greater funds. Negotiating a reasonable, sound agreement quickly and establishing a positive relationship between Pathogenesis and the University of Washington yielded ample financial returns and formed strong relationships.

NEGOTIATIONS

What factors lead to problematic relations between universities and companies?

The first hurdle is prolonged negotiations over terms, which most frequently involve IP terms. It is critical to realize that the value of much technology is fleeting and that there are narrow temporal windows of opportunity to exploit research results. In addition, budget cycles for company expenditures frequently have finite periods, and if the funds are not committed, they are lost for a particular project. Therefore, it is essential that university spokesmen quickly establish the university's needs and limitations and to politely withdraw if a company has expectations that cannot be met. Faculty must be educated beforehand about suitable terms and conditions, so that during their marketing they don't raise unrealistic expectations in the company sponsor. Faculty are extremely busy and frequently their time is overcommitted. Consequently, they are only interested in rules and regulations on a need-to-know basis. Faculty willingly listen to explanations of rules and regulations with regard to management of hazardous materials, animal care, and human subjects in their early days of the academy because they need permission and certification in these areas to conduct their research. But the policies regarding university-industry affairs are of little interest until a potential agreement is in the offing. It is crucial, therefore, that the university establish timely, cost-effective programs to educate faculty on university-industry affairs.

There is a useful phrase that senior administrators can employ when discussing impasses with companies: "I'm sorry, but we are unable to do that ... " Not that we are unwilling or displeased to do that but we are unable to do that. One of the actions that universities are unable to do is to indemnify companies. These legal obligations are beyond most universities' risk tolerance. No university has the financial capability to manage product liability. In addition, universities have no control over manufacture of company products. Universities are also unable to restrict publication of research results. A limited set of other such terms arise and university counsel can be helpful here. Finally, company representatives must know that universities have public obligations such as disclosure and tax laws that companies do not have and, unlike industry, universities are not protected by the concept of bankruptcy.

Intellectual property terms have become a flash point in university-industry affairs, particularly with the industries considered to be heavily vested in developing information technology (IT) companies. Universities frequently wish to preserve their freedom to negotiate IP terms for licensing until after the research is concluded and when faculty have made disclosures about the IP. It is a reasonable desire, because one doesn't know in advance what specific results, technologies, or disclosures will arise. In addition, it may not always be clear what other sources of funding may have supported the disclosed material.

Companies have a reasonable expectation for use at a reasonable price of the results they supported. The company perspective, on the one hand, is that the price paid is the direct and indirect costs collected by the university in the course of the research. This view rarely considers funds contributed as background research in the accounting. Universities, on the other hand, frequently overestimate the value of the information delivered and underestimate the costs involved in developing the results obtained into a viable commercial product. In fact, except for a blockbuster drug derived from a university patent, it frequently is difficult to determine the value of a resulting technology and therefore to set a proper license fee on it. It may also be difficult to determine how to collect! For example, in the IT industry it may be problematic to collect on an enhancement of a component of a product that is part of a system. If a company wishes a technology "to be managed" by the university, however, then compensation beyond indirect costs is essential. Management of IP takes time and effort.

Few can foresee or estimate the monetary value of a result arising from research or the cost of developing it into a useful product or service. A good starting point is for the company to have internal use rights or to pay some set fee to exercise nonexclusive rights to the technology. Most often the biggest advantages for the commercial uses of technologies emerge through early development that enhances a competitive advantage. This is best promoted by the university through thoughtful transfer of the technology to the company. The transfer process is essentially one of teaching the technology in great detail to the company.

One of the biggest problems caused by poor relations between a university and a company is a secret deal whereby the company gives a "gift" for the research in exchange for a private understanding with faculty. The company then obtains intimate knowledge, hidden results, and excellent teaching of the results through paid consulting fees to the principal faculty. Participating graduate students are the big losers in this instance because their intellectual property mysteriously disappears. Subsequent allegations of misconduct—via graduate students blowing the whistle and the public finding that its interest is not being served—can be problematic for all concerned. In addition, such circumstances may threaten the tax status of the university under IRS regulations.

Confidentiality agreements between universities and companies can also pose a problem. Open communication in a collegial environment makes retention of confidential information almost impossible from a practical, policy, or philosophical standpoint. The university has no mechanism for insuring, maintaining, or enforcing confidentiality terms in most environments. Multiyear terms for confidentiality don't make much sense for the university to undertake, when graduate students may be gone in a matter of months. Consequently, it is best that the university avoid projects where confidential company information is essential for the work unless the agreement is on the usual best-efforts or reasonable-efforts basis and is restricted to the principle investigators.

Restricting publication of research results is counter to the university mission and general character and is a "deal breaker." Restricting publication is construed as jeopardizing graduate education and collegiality and strikes at the core of university values—moreover, it undermines public confidence and support. Delaying publication may be acceptable for limited periods of time in order to review manuscripts for possible protection of intellectual property. In rare circumstances, extended delays can be managed in order to provide for examination of large data sets as long as the delay does not interfere with the graduation of students.

Indemnification, tight retention of confidential information, and review of publication with a right to restrict publication are all examples of terms that universities usually are "unable" to accept in a normal, open environment. It is beneficial for universities to establish these conditions at the onset of discussions with companies. If confidentiality is required, one way to manage it is by providing special facilities that restrict access and are secure. This usually means special buildings or floors. Obviously, it is imperative to maintain comprehensive publication of results in this circumstance to avoid allegations regarding the conduct of "secret" research.

Students have increasingly higher expectations regarding intellectual property that they have generated as part of their education. This is so whether the IP is patentable, software, or know-how. Expectations may include a desire to form a start-up company on the basis of the IP. It is important, therefore, that they understand the terms and conditions of industry-sponsored agreements that support their studies. In this context, it may be important to ensure that agreements ("participation agreements") are signed by all students, faculty, and staff working on a company-sponsored project acknowledging and agreeing to the terms of the agreement before they initiate work. Participation agreements are vital when the company may exercise rights to IP arising. Students should be under no illusions regarding the potential use of these rights in starting a company.

Stock equity positions in start-up companies have become a valuable means of protecting the public interest in the commercialization of university-based IP and in providing downstream income for support of research. Universities should be cautious, however, of the nature of sponsored research from companies in which the university has an equity position, particularly in a privately held company that has emerged as a university-related start-up.

It is critical that the university uphold its reputation as an impartial, unbiased provider of research results. Although the university may manage some conflict-of-interest circumstances when a faculty member has an equity interest in a company, some conflicts are not manageable and some perceptions of conflict cannot be tolerated. Research involving clinical trials is a case in point. Under no circumstances should the university enter into sponsored research that involves clinical research with a private company in which the university or the PI has an equity position. It has been argued that under rare circumstances the clinicians who founded the company are the only persons capable of conducting the appropriate clinical studies. If that were true, then the faculty should teach the appropriate technology to clinicians at another university so that the second university can conduct the research at arm's length. Alternatively, the university and faculty can give up their equity positions. Otherwise, perceptions and allegations of misconduct and conflict of interest undermine the credibility and reputation of those involved and the university. The same may be said of technologies affecting the environment or public safety. The university and its faculty must be seen to be above reproach; equity positions undermine this view.

ROLE OF UNIVERSITY ADMINISTRATORS

Within a university, the role of technology managers in negotiating university-industry agreements is different from the role of grants administrators that manage federal and foundation grants.

A dissimilar approach to faculty and companies is important. Consequently, a divergent skill set is essential. The first difference is that a university-industry agreement is a deal that must be negotiated as discussed above. The technology manager must have excellent communication skills to convince both the faculty and company when fundamental university policy is involved. Grants administrators have almost no freedom of movement and no one expects them to negotiate with the federal government or foundations regarding rules and regulations. They cannot "give in" or compromise anything. For the most part they follow rules. But companies expect universities to adjust desirable terms in order to close a deal. A second major difference is dealing with uncertain time frames, budgets, and deliverables. With the federal government, time frames are rigid, budgets are established by form, and deliverables are for the most part publications and reports. A third difference involves complicated legal issues, some of which are outlined above, and reference to legal counsel is sometimes important when negotiating university-industry agreements as the deal is established in a contract. All of these factors lead to a need for judgment and significant experience. Therefore, training, support, and retention of successful technology managers are a major issue.

The role of the vice president, vice provost, or vice chancellor of research is also a critical element in university-industry agreements and relations. Any one of these administrators may be called upon to clarify an ambiguous point in policy or to be a key person convincing faculty and companies of an element of an agreement that the university is unable to enforce or implement. In a large university with a number of agreements, it has become useful to appoint a senior faculty member as a vice provost with the sole responsibility for university-industry affairs, without the additional burden of administration of federal grants and research infrastructure. This enables the vice provost to specialize and to be available on a constant basis to aid in managing and closing deals. This person provides important support for the technology managers in dealing with both companies and faculty. The companies frequently appreciate having a high-level university administrator as a point of contact, and faculty often look only to another faculty member for final adjudication of ambiguity and disagreement.

Summary

The following take-home points are essential in university-industry agreements:

- Relationship building is a key aspect of industry-sponsored research.
- Faculty are the critical driver of the process.
- Deliverables to the company are important and must be understood by all.
- Negotiations should be timely and companies should be informed of university limitations early in the process of discussion.
- Some stock equity positions and sponsored research don't mix.

CHAPTER THREE

IS TECHNOLOGY TRANSFER A WINNING PROPOSITION?

Katharine Ku

A university must have a clear set of principles upon which to make financial and licensing decisions. At Stanford University, our philosophy is to base all licensing decisions on doing what is best for the technology and to nurture the development of as many licensing seeds as possible. We have learned that: (1) technology transfer is not about "the money"—it is about good relationships with researchers, with companies, and with the community at large; (2) technology transfer is complex and there are no easy answers; and (3) the rewards take a long time in coming and patience is the name of the game.

Technology transfer is the movement of knowledge and discoveries from the university to the public. It occurs in many ways, such as through journal publications, graduated students, exchanges at scientific conferences, and informal and formal relationships with industry. For the purposes of this chapter, technology transfer (also commonly known as "tech transfer") refers to the formal licensing of university technology and intellectual property to industry.

Because the Bayh-Dole law of 1980 allows universities to have ownership rights to discoveries resulting from federally funded research, universities throughout the United States have become involved in technology transfer activities. Universities have many reasons to participate in technology transfer activities, for example, to commercialize university inventions via the Bayh-Dole law, facilitate faculty recruitment and retention, engage in economic development, and pursue royalty income on behalf of faculty and the university.

The Bayh-Dole law, however, does not require a university to generate any royalty income at all. Indeed, technology transfer—and economic development—can occur independently of royalty income. Although most university technology transfer personnel agree that their work is not about "the money," university administrations are always interested in the financial aspects of such operations. Therefore, based on our thirty-six years of experience at Stanford University, I address the question of whether technology transfer is a viable and reliable source of income for a university.

TECHNOLOGY TRANSFER PRACTICE AND "BUSINESS"

It is hard for a university technology transfer office to be a true "business" within a university environment. For example, if a university wants to *maximize* royalty revenue, then the "financial bottom line" would almost always determine the course of action for a particular licensing transaction. Even if a university only wanted to *optimize* royalty revenue, then the financial bottom line would determine the outcome most of the time. In most licensing situations within the university, however, the bottom line cannot be the determining factor because there are too many other factors to take into consideration.

University technology transfer practices are complex, often requiring the delicate balancing of opposing goals. For example, many administrators would like tech transfer to be a service function to the faculty-researchers in order to encourage them to disclose inventions and work with the tech transfer office. A truly business-focused office, however, would want to spend time and resources only on money-making transactions, which would mean that many, if not most, faculty would not be served.

From a business perspective, it is not always clear whether it is financially better to license a start-up or an existing company, if there is a choice (most often not the case!). By definition, start-ups do not have much cash. They are inherently very risky because they often have novice management, limited resources, minimal experience, technical challenges, and market competition. Most tech transfer offices have come to realize that they can't rely solely on start-up activity for financial returns. However, although it may be more lucrative financially to license to an existing company that may have more financial resources, such companies often have so many competing projects that they do not devote enough time and effort to developing the university invention.

Licensing decisions and transactions require the balancing of opposing principles. For example, exclusive licenses may be necessary to encourage development of an invention, and yet, nonexclusive licenses would allow many companies to exploit an invention with the potential of a bigger royalty stream because, ostensibly, the pie is bigger. Although the decision about exclusivity depends on the stage of development of the invention and the time and resources needed to bring the invention to the marketplace, these factors are often subjective because no one really knows the technical and market risks involved in commercializing the invention. Thus, it is not always clear whether it is better to "put all your eggs in one basket" (the "exclusive" model) or "spread the risk" (the "nonexclusive" model) when trying to optimize or maximize revenue.

Finally, another area particular to university technology transfer is the complex relationship with inventors. Unlike most corporate employees, university inventors have a financial stake in the outcome of any licensing transaction (as mandated by Bayh-Dole). Because many inventors feel that "their" invention should be under "their" control, licensing offices generally consider the input of the inventors before deciding on a licensing strategy, thus affecting the financial outcome of a licensing transaction. Some inventors have strong opinions about which company is or is not an appropriate licensee, which is sometimes contrary to the views of the licensing office. Inventor involvement in the actual transfer of know-how and information greatly enhances the chance of successful commercialization, and thus the inventor's input is important but can be a very complicating factor at the same time. The one guiding principle for any director to keep in mind is that decisions—particularly with respect to inventors—create "precedence," and so each decision must be made with the awareness that one will face the issue again, in a different or similar context, and that consistency in dealing with inventors is very important.

UNIVERSITY TECHNOLOGY TRANSFER CHALLENGES

Amid the ambivalent and contradictory elements in a university technology transfer office, the biggest challenge is simply that every invention is different and involves a custom approach. Most inventions are early stage and undeveloped. The potential licenses are all different. Industry sectors vary widely in their attitude toward university licensing, but a university can be assured that no matter what the industry, the company wants to pay as little as possible for a license. Inventor relationships are unique—some inventors want to control as much as possible while others do not want to be involved or bothered with business issues. Intellectual property protection is varied and often unpredictable, taking a long time and much money for a patent to eventually issue.

Another complicating factor is that constituents may want different outcomes. Here are several examples.

- Although inventors may hope for maximum royalty income, students and faculty often have different time perspectives on short-term versus long-term cash flow. For example, is it better to have a bigger up-front payment in exchange for a lower royalty stream, or vice versa? Inventors may also disagree on the best course for commercialization of the technology.
- The university administration wants to generate royalty income with minimal effort, cost, and controversy, and without perturbing the research enterprise.
- The U.S. government wants the technology to be transferred but imposes restrictions on how certain research tool technologies, such as the NIH Guidelines on Research Tools, should be transferred. Moreover, if universities are too successful (make too much money), the government threatens to take a portion of the royalties.

- Companies differ. Their interest and emphases depend on whether they are focused on life sciences or physical sciences, and their sizes vary enormously. Multinational companies tend to want nonexclusive freedom-of-action licenses while start-up companies want as much exclusivity as possible. Semiconductor, telecommunications, and information technology companies believe in cross-licensing and freedom-to-operate licensing whereas life sciences companies often prefer exclusive licenses. Many IT companies typically want to have fully paid (lump sum) licenses because they do not want to pay royalties on sales; other companies (such as life sciences companies) prefer to pay earned royalties when they have the certainty of sales. The variations in industry-wide and individual corporate attitudes require that licensing offices be flexible in order to be effective.

THE STANFORD STRATEGY

With so many conflicting goals and constituencies, a university must have a clear set of principles upon which to make financial and licensing decisions. At Stanford, we try to base all licensing decisions on doing what is best for the technology; we have a strong philosophy of nurturing the development of as many licensing seeds as possible. In order to put Stanford's licensing program into context, a few statistics on Stanford's research enterprise are useful:

In FY2005–06, U.S. government funding of research—excluding the Stanford Linear Accelerator Center (SLAC)—was approximately $600 million. (SLAC is funded by the Department of Defense and generates very few inventions.) The total budget for sponsored research, including SLAC, is about $1 billion. Corporate sponsorship, which includes clinical trial sponsors, was $35 million. An estimated 4,000 graduate students and 1,100 faculty are involved in research. We have a strong medical and engineering school, as well as solid biology, chemistry, and physics disciplines. The number of invention disclosures per year has been steadily rising with over four hundred disclosures in 2005 and over five hundred disclosures in 2006, typically divided equally between physical science and life sciences inventions.

A brief summary of the high points of the Stanford technology transfer efforts is revealing. The good news is that during our thirty-six-year history (fiscal years 1970–2006), we received over 6,400 invention-technology disclosures and we generated over $1 billion in royalty revenue. Excluding our top three greatest royalty generators as of the end of the 2006 fiscal year (Google with over $335 million to date; the Cohen-Boyer patents with $255 million for Stanford and the University of California; and Functional Antibody with $125 million), $345 million has been received for "all other inventions." It is sobering to note that three inventions generated 67 percent of the cumulative income.

It should be noted that it took Stanford fifteen years to "break even," defined as our 15 percent administrative fee covering our office budget. Part of any office's potential for success depends on the number of years it has been in existence.

Out of 6,400 inventions in thirty-six years, only three of them were "big winners," defined as having generated $50 million or more in cumulative royalty revenue. Of the 6,400 inventions, 16 have generated $5 million in cumulative revenue; 53 have generated $1 million or more in cumulative revenue; and 287 inventions have made $100,000 or more.

The most notable statistic is that 80 percent of disclosed inventions did not bring in any revenue. In general, however, 90 percent of the licensed inventions brought in enough revenue to cover patent expenses.

Evaluating a Technology Transfer Office

How good a job is a technology transfer office doing? Again, the answer is complex.

Royalty Revenue

Many look to royalty revenue as a measure of performance. A vital point about royalty figures, however, is that the royalty stream in any one year is mostly dependent on license agreements entered into in the past. In other words, the royalty revenue does not reflect how well the office is currently doing in transferring new technology. In general, Stanford's new license agreements (which is the measure of the current year's productivity) and their associated "up-front royalty fees" contribute about 5 percent to the year's overall revenue. For example, in 2005–06, we signed 109 new license agreements wherein the up-front payments due in 2005–06 (approximately $3.2 million) amounted to 5 percent of the $61.3 million in that year's overall royalty revenue.

INVENTION QUALITY

An office's ability to transfer technology effectively depends to a great extent on the quality and stage of development of the inventions, and the industry to which the inventions are applicable. Physical science inventions are normally considered harder to license than life science inventions. Later-stage technology is easier to license than very early stage inventions. If a working prototype or clinical data exist, the invention is more licensable. These factors are beyond the control of technology transfer staff but make a big difference in an office's ability to license the technology.

CUSTOMER SATISFACTION

Notwithstanding the factors that are beyond an office's control, a large part of the perceived effectiveness of the technology transfer office depends on the staff's ability to work well with faculty and industry. At Stanford, we are always evaluating our performance with respect to customer satisfaction, using customer surveys to collect feedback from inventors and licensees. If an inventor is disgruntled, we are able to address this issue immediately. The area most often needing attention is keeping the inventor informed about the status of the invention. If an inventor feels involved and informed, he or she will work better with the office, and in turn, the office will be perceived as being effective. Likewise, we hope that licensees feel that we negotiated the license in a reasonable time and that the ultimate agreement is considered a fair arrangement.

METRICS

In addition to qualitative evaluations, we use quantitative measurements to assess performance. We track the number of new licenses per year, or "New Monies" in our terminology, the number of inventions handled per licensing professional, and a subjective per-person productivity measure. A typical caseload is at least 250–300 inventions per licensing team (a professional and an assistant) which include portfolios of inventions that can be handled under one licensing program or commercialization strategy. Of course, a licensing person specializing in software or biological materials may have a lesser caseload because he or she does not have administrative assistance. It is clear that life sciences inventions are easier to license than physical science inventions because the life science companies are more amenable to licensing. Typically, one licensing person in the life sciences arena can do 10–20 new licenses per year. In contrast, a licensing person in the physical sciences arena can typically complete fewer licenses, approximately 4–8 new licenses in one year. In all cases, the number of licenses per person depends on the quality of the invention and the particular industry sector. To reiterate, the Stanford office philosophy is to "plant as many licensing seeds as possible," which is why we measure the number of seeds that we plant.

NEW LICENSES

During an average "good year" of licensing (not our best year, not our worst), thirteen licensing professionals concluded 109 new licenses. The technologies run the gamut from nonpatented biomaterial and biotech, which accounts for half of the total, to software, instruments, medical, chemistry, semiconductor, copyright, nanotechnology, photonics, high-energy physics, and so on. The majority of licenses (62.4 percent) are nonexclusive where the technologies are licensed to more than one company; 25 percent are exclusive licenses and the remaining 13 percent are options to license. One-third of the companies are large and publicly held although many small companies, including start-ups, are licensed. Up-front fees payable in the fiscal year, once the license is signed, range from a few thousand dollars up to $400,000 (this does not include money due in the future). The percentage equity in start-up licenses is typically 5 percent or less.

Table 3.1 shows nine years of "New Monies" data. It is clear that a year-by-year tally shows great variation in the number of licenses signed per year. To us, it seems that the economy plays a large part in industry's receptivity to technology licensing. We have worked hard to do as few "zero-dollar" licenses as possible and to increase the number of agreements whose up-front fee is more than $10,000, certainly more than $5,000! Nevertheless, the median of all these years is still $10,000 or less.

PATENT EXPENSES

It is easy to run up a large patent expense bill. A university must decide how much to allocate for patents and how much risk it is willing to incur. As of the end of FY2006, Stanford had an inventory of $8 million in unlicensed patents or patent applications. We typically write off between $500,000 to $1 million every year for inventions (inventory) that we have not been able to license. That is, we deem the invention to be unlicensable and repay the General Fund the patent expenses from our 15 percent administrative fee. Based on our current database of 2,300 active inventions, we filed patents on almost 70 percent of our disclosures (the percentage is high because we have dropped many of the inventions on which we did not file patents) and licensed about 32 percent of those disclosures (many of them not patented at all). Of our 1,590 active inventions which have been patented, 46 percent are licensed.

The management of patents and their expenses is not straightforward. Some inventions ripen with age and get better; others become less commercially viable over time. Most university inventions are early stage, and companies must be willing to undertake both technical and market risks in order to attempt to commercialize an invention. Thus, each licensing professional has to decide whether or not to keep incurring patent expenses on any particular unlicensed invention. We do not have any hard-and-fast rules about which patents to maintain or drop; each professional has to make the decision constantly as prosecution expenses or maintenance fees mount up. A "guideline" for making that decision

TABLE 3.1. STATISTICS ON NEW LICENSES (NEW MONIES) AT STANFORD UNIVERSITY DURING A NINE-YEAR PERIOD

	1997–1998	1998–1999	1999–2000	2000–2001	2001–2002	2002–2003	2003–2004	2004–2005	2005–2006
New licenses	119	147	162	137	113	127	89	84	109
Equity	$3,283,814	$3,716,250	$2,671,550	$3,044,000	$1,419,000	$2,592,000	$1,246,700	$1,194,290	$3,249,107
Up-Front Fees									
None	4	5	15	22	11	13	10	4	5
Under $5K	18	21	40	31	29	35	22	21	33
Under $10K	43	60	86	57	52	70	48	39	50
$10K and over	76	87	76	80	61	58	41	45	59
Type of Agreement									
Nonexclusive		84	106	84	64	81	53	46	68
Exclusive		44	31	36	27	31	27	23	27
Option		19	25	17	22	16	9	15	14
Subsets of Above									
Licenses involving equity	7	17	20	16	13	17	9	12	10
Ready to sign agreements		5	32	21	4	7	5	3	3
License back to inventor			5	5	4	2	10	1	5
Inventor pays patent costs			1	1	0	1	0	0	0

is that the licensing professional has to believe the technology can be licensed for more than the expenses incurred in order to keep spending money on that particular invention. Typically, cumulative expenses of $30,000 or more on an invention warrant additional scrutiny and justification and the licensing staff are keenly aware of the "negative balances" for their cases, both cumulatively and individually.

Some universities would say that it is fiscally necessary and responsible to have a patent budget so that the university knows what its patent liability will be in any one year. The disadvantage of a fixed patent budget is that it is hard to know how to spend the funds because the inventions come in at unpredictable times of the year. The best invention may come in at the end of the year when all the money has been spent. Alternatively, an office may file patents just to spend the budgeted amount for that year, even if the inventions are only marginally commercially viable. At Stanford, the General Fund prepays the patent expenses, and Stanford's Office of Technology Licensing (OTL) repays the General Fund when the technology is licensed or dropped. We have essentially a "revolving line of credit" without a set patent budget. Because OTL has been careful about its patent expenditures and has been successful in licensing technologies, OTL has been able to "pay off the revolving line of credit to the General Fund" over the years and is currently paying for all patent expenses through the OTL 15 percent administrative fee.

STAFFING

Staffing needs depend on a university's philosophy, goals, ambition, and resources. The questions that each university should consider include:

1. Do you want to just pick "potential winners" or license as many technologies as possible? On the one hand, if the staff only works on "potential winners," each professional will have fewer inventions to concentrate on but will be able to delve deeper into the markets and industries. On the other hand, if the philosophy is to license as many technologies as possible, the staff will be

responsible for many technologies with a limited ability to spend much time with any one of them.

2. What is the university attitude toward start-ups and how much and in what ways does it want to help entrepreneurs, if at all? Typically, there are a limited number of university technologies which can be the basis of a solid stand-alone new company and it takes tremendous time and effort to launch a new company start-up. The type of person who has the appropriate experience to mentor a start-up often has different qualifications from a person who licenses technology. The "start-up" mentor will not have time to do many licenses.

3. How much marketing or outreach should the office do? How committed is the university to the concept of fair and open access? Should the office license the first interested party or try to ensure that as many companies as possible have been exposed to the offer of a license before granting an exclusive license? Marketing broadly to many potential licensees takes more time and effort than if an office is willing to license the first company who expresses interest.

4. Do you prefer exclusive or nonexclusive licensing? A nonexclusive license program often takes more time initially in order to establish terms and conditions that will be fair and attractive to many companies. In addition, a nonexclusive licensing program generally puts the onus of patent protection and enforcement on the university. An exclusive license relies on the capabilities of that particular licensee—you are "putting all your eggs in one basket" and thus the licensee's diligent development is the key to success. Different skills are sometimes needed for different kinds of licensing strategies.

5. Do you want to plant licensing seeds or nurture seedlings? Again, as in points one and two above, nurturing seedlings take much more time than planting licensing seeds. "Nurturing" requires putting more vested time and effort into a company whereas typical licensing arrangements rely on the licensee to develop the product.

The answers to these questions will help determine how many staff members you need and what kind of qualifications they should have in order to run an effective office.

Equity

Many universities focus on start-ups and the equity component of a license agreement, feeling that equity is where the revenue will come from, because a royalty stream could take many years to develop before a product is introduced into the marketplace. Stanford's philosophy has always been that equity is just one part of the consideration in a license—and not the most important component. Stanford has taken equity in almost two hundred companies and, excluding Google, has cashed out approximately $24 million. (Google was an anomaly in large part because its price per share was so high and should not be taken as a representative example of typical equity cash out.)

Disclosures

Universities often wonder if they are getting a reasonable number of disclosures for their research enterprise. One general rule of thumb is that one might expect about one invention disclosure per $2 million in research funding. Stanford tracks fairly closely to that ratio. In our portfolio of active cases, about 10 percent are being evaluated, about 40 percent are being marketed to potential licensees, and 50 percent have been licensed either exclusively or nonexclusively.

Legal Review

Stanford's Office of the General Counsel is not required to review any of the license agreements and the OTL director signs all of them. Nevertheless, OTL works closely with the Office of the General Counsel on legal matters and is not hesitant to confer with our lawyers if necessary or appropriate. The OTL is well aware of its duty to minimize risk and legal exposure.

Management

Operationally, the licensing professionals in OTL have considerable autonomy to negotiate terms and conditions of a license. They are closest to the inventors and licensees and know the technology the best. They are responsible for marketing the technology, making patenting decisions, and determining the structure, pricing, and actual wording of the license agreement. The OTL director signs all license agreements.

ATTITUDE

In general, Stanford OTL strives to be known as a reasonable, flexible, and action-oriented office. From a financial negotiation standpoint, Stanford is prepared to be reasonable in light of the particular issues or special considerations that a potential licensee brings forward. We recognize that the technology and market risks are usually unknown for most inventions and that the license agreement is the basis of a long-term relationship. We believe that having a good relationship is the most important aspect of a successful licensing program. If the licensee can be successful, the presumption is that Stanford will share in the licensee's success.

SUMMARY AND CONCLUSIONS

Is technology transfer a winning proposition? It can be, but only if one is thoughtful about the finances and is patient, careful, supportive, and realistic. In addition, the mission and the operations of the technology transfer office must be clear to the university community. Most important, technology transfer can be a winning proposition if the university defines "winning" in the broadest perspective, not only in terms of finances, but also in terms of enhanced reputation, good relationships with faculty, students and alumni, and good relationships with companies, big and small.

Chapter Four

Digital Ventures

Managing Software-Based Research Assets

Charles R. Williams and Gerald Barnett

Digital Ventures at the University of Washington generated nearly $40 million in licensing income from digital assets, returning 40 percent to laboratory project budgets to support industry relationships. In doing so, Digital Ventures created a technology transfer program in alignment with the research and instructional objectives of our faculty. The models developed by Digital Ventures address common objections to patent-based licensing programs, operate across campus, and demonstrate a viable alternative approach to innovation management.

Digital Ventures

In 1989, Dr. Alvin Kwiram, the vice provost for research at the University of Washington, started an experiment in technology transfer that led to the development of one of the country's top intellectual property groups specializing in academic software. The question was whether software intellectual property could be managed productively in a university technology transfer program. The answer was a resounding yes. The effort has taught us important lessons about the social dynamics of academic innovation, the relationship of research exchange to commercial markets, strategies for developing relationships with industry scientists and engineers, and how our activities grow the research enterprise.

Sixteen years of experimentation and adaptation over the course of changing political, economic, and social forces have shaped the philosophy and practice of software transfer at the University of Washington. The organization has gone by various names since its inception—Software Transfer, Software and Copyright Ventures, and most recently, Digital Ventures. Digital Ventures presently operates as a unit of the University of Washington's TechTransfer organization, reporting to the vice provost for intellectual property and technology transfer. From the start, Digital Ventures took a flexible, if not contrarian, approach to intellectual property management. Since its formation, Digital Ventures has managed over five hundred projects and has grown to an office of 5.25 licensing professionals, a contract manager, and a half-time administrative assistant. It engages faculty, staff, and students campuswide in discussions about open access to research results, software distribution, and economic development in Washington State through start-up creation.

THE MULTIPLICITOUS NATURE OF SOFTWARE

We should be clear at the outset what we mean by "software." In a university context, "software" encompasses a wide range of computer programs, databases, research data stored in electronic forms, World Wide Web and digital media works, documentation, performance and technical data, and software development environments. Many of these works are developed to support research or instruction, but others are developed to support administrative functions. Often university software works are only partly developed—sufficient to provide a function to a lab, or to demonstrate a concept—and few are polished enough to be called "products." One of the first challenges in managing software, therefore, is recognizing that the work to be "transferred" is not in the form of products to be sold, but rather as an intermediate stage in an ongoing process of development. For most university software assets, the distributable form is that of a "tool," "platform," or "artifact."

In terms of structure and intellectual property, software is also a composite of works, formats, and rights. Software usually involves multiple assets, developed over time by a number of contributors, following multiple forms of intellectual property. Software consists of "source code"—relatively readable program statements—and "object code," generated from the source code in a format necessary for a computer to process the statements, or to "run" the software. In most contexts, any particular software "work" may be comprised of multiple modules or works, each with multiple copyrights, trademarks, and patent rights available, along with rights in data (trade secrets) and quasi-intellectual property rights such as personal publicity and privacy rights (in the case of using identifiable personal likenesses, voice talent, or biographical information) and domain names (in the case of Internet applications). In practice, software is not an "it" but rather a "them"—consisting of multiple assets that must be handled collectively.

THE UNEASY FIT OF SOFTWARE IN TECHNOLOGY TRANSFER OFFICES

In a conventional technology transfer office, software is likely to be "handled like any other invention"—that is, "disclosed," evaluated for "commercial potential" and possible patent rights, and if one or more companies appear to have an interest, patent applications may be filed and efforts made to license the technology to industry for development. Software management, however, is usually tightly coupled with scholarly collaboration and communication. For most university software, patent rights are the least relevant among the forms of intellectual property controls, and finding a company to sell their software as a commercial product is often low on academic software developers' lists of objectives.

A common mistake made by technology transfer offices is to adopt a "product" approach for what appears to be reasonably mature software. Whether an office distributes directly or seeks a commercial distributor, the "product" approach fails to capture the value of relationships and attribution desired by faculty. Along with a host of potential support, legal, and tax issues to navigate, this approach appears "corporate," and users expect the technology transfer office and faculty to operate as if they were software vendors. Lost in such an approach are the collaborative relationships that form the core of university software development. Technology transfer offices and their university software developers are poorly prepared to handle the challenges of acting as industry software vendors, and it is therefore no surprise that software developers are among the most strident critics of university patent licensing offices that fail to deliver on promises beyond what they are able to deliver.

From the software development perspective, patent-based technology transfer is a huge problem. Technology transfer offices interfere with research collaboration, undermine leadership positions with delays and bureaucracy, create bitterness over ownership and money, interfere with industry collaborations, incur needless patenting expenses, do not support programmers' needs, assert control points indiscriminately, and do not understand collaborative development and standards. These are just a few of the objections. University leaders should not underestimate the depth of dislike and frustration that software developers feel toward their conventional, invention-based technology transfer offices and policy that treats software differently from "traditional scholarly works." One can compel developers to follow an invention and patent process ill suited to software practice and objectives, treating software like any other invention, or one can create new programs that support software deployment on its own terms.

Most of the time, university-developed software is incomplete, workable for a relatively narrow set of purposes. As developers say, academic software is not "hardened" for customer or commercial use, meaning that it tends not to be tested on a range of systems, checked for compatibility with different hardware configurations, quality checked for "bugs" in the code or documentation, or checked for compliance with industry standards. In fact, one of the premises of "open source" software is that the user community may provide development and support services to correct problems and develop extensions in desirable directions. This makes software management a nightmare—or irrelevant—for technology transfer offices accustomed to inventions that can be delineated by one or more patent applications prepared by legal professionals.

COPYRIGHT LEADS TO "SOFTWARE IS DIFFERENT"

We have found that experience with copyright and trademark is valued in university units that are not otherwise likely to participate in invention-based work. We formed the Copyright Network to bring together for brown bag lunch meetings faculty, staff, and students with interests in copyright from across the institution, including the libraries, computing and communications, and other administrative units. As we became involved in discussions of fair use, ownership, pending legislation, distance education, online reserves, and the cost of scholarly journals, we saw that copyright management matters to many more people in the university than does patent management. We also saw that copyright and trademark issues were seen largely as a drag on patent licensing operations—a necessary "service" to the faculty to be subsidized from patent licensing revenues, but not expected to be of any particular consequence.

Working with copyrights taught us that software had much more potential than that perceived by an invention-based view of the world. Where there were no patent rights, we found university developers committed to their programs and we found receptive industry audiences willing to support these programs. Whether the software was offered without formalities, with an open source license, or under a more formal contractual regime, the focus of attention was the beneficial exchange between a lab and its community, not the rights that went along with the transactions.

Digital Ventures dealt with the complexity of software by developing the concept of the "project" as distinct from an "invention disclosure." A project is a cluster of people, information technology, and intangible assets (including intellectual property) coordinated to support development, distribution, use, and instruction of the project's assets. The project internally organizes the development team and their contributions, and coordinates the relationships that the team develops with recipients of software. A project is analogous to a start-up enterprise, formed under the rules of the university to carry out a university mission, much as a sponsored research agreement establishes a principal investigator and supervised personnel, all bound by common obligations to fulfill the conditions of the external award. A project has a director, a roster of personnel who acknowledge their obligations to the project, a financial arrangement for management of income from distribution activities, and a working relationship with Digital Ventures.

A Classroom of Companies

The fundamental question of conventional university technology transfer is: "Does this invention have commercial value protected by available patent rights?" For Digital Ventures, the fundamental question is radically different: "Should this technology represented by this cluster of software assets be taught to capable audiences?" This difference is critical to the success of Digital Ventures. Although there is continuing debate over whether universities should be involved in patent licensing, there is broad consensus that universities should be committed to instruction, and that it is entirely appropriate for universities to generate revenue to support this activity. From the outset, Digital Ventures has been committed to aligning its practices with the university's research and instructional missions, rather than operating on the margin as a discretionary-fund generator under the premise of public service.

Software transfer is best managed as an instructional activity with intellectual property significance. The goal is to create a "classroom of companies"—organizations with an interest in learning how new software tools operate rather than staying in the dark. There is no need for a commercial product phase, or even the involvement of for-profit companies to distribute the software. Software assets are valued for their information content and the relationship they can establish between recipients and the project. In this manner, intellectual property in software management does not "protect" the software. Unlike most university patent practices, the value of software is not in the opportunity to exclude others from using it; rather, the value is in the extent to which the software is *used*, especially in the earliest interactions, and the degree to which the software creates a user and shared development community. Intellectual property for university-developed software is useful primarily—if not solely—as a relationship tool to shape early relationships, attract investment, and manage quality.

The objectives of software distribution are to build working relationships (an intangible asset), create goodwill (an attribute of trademark), enhance program visibility (also an attribute of trademark), generate resources for projects (monetary, but also referral of opportunity, in-kind contributions, and access to expertise), and enhance the experience for students involved in our projects (contacts with recipient organizations, valuable research problems, placement). Following this model, Digital Ventures has helped variously to release software without charge, start companies that have attracted substantial venture investment, and generate millions in funding for support of software projects.

The Bayh-Dole Act is broadly credited with establishing university technology transfer practice. What is often lost is that Bayh-Dole's emphasis is on the use of the patent system to encourage "practical application" of inventions so that their benefits are made available to the public. As patent-based technology licensing offices have demonstrated, one way to do this is to stimulate the development of commercial products to be sold to customers. Bayh-Dole does not, however, require this approach. Digital Ventures emphasizes the importance of "practical application" by building collaborative relationships with industry. Digital Ventures aims to establish research communities in both nonprofit and industry settings. From there, if the community develops the software, there may be opportunities to encourage internal operational use at companies, and then, potentially, to development of commercial products. For software to gain value, it has to be used, early and often. Developers need to work with an audience of users to plan a roadmap for further work with the code. This interaction is at the heart of developing high-quality research tools—and high-quality relationships. These relationships are based on instruction, not licenses.

INTERNET DISTRIBUTION OF ASSETS

If finding capable audiences to instruct is a fundamental goal, how do we connect a project with the rest of the world? Sometimes all that is needed is to post the software to a Web site. But at other times, this is neither effective nor appropriate (and results in what some call "abandonware"—unsupported code adrift and ignored). Sometimes greater attention is needed to support software deployment, even among academics. Information technology has heavily impacted our practice. Over seventy-five hundred licenses were executed through our portal last year; most were click-through licenses that provide (a) metrics and attribution for our faculty and students and (b) filters for managing access to appropriate audiences (academic, health care professionals, contributors, and the like). Fee-based licensing has been facilitated by the Internet, particularly for licenses carrying modest fees that do not typically require cost justification and acceptance steps in the receiving organization.

Some of Digital Venture's most valuable software has had little or no commercial potential, and yet has been of tremendous value to the university. The Pine (now alPine) messaging software system, for instance, is known around the world and has been used by twenty-nine million users. Pine is made available at no charge, with the source code available for local modification. You can expect to find Pine on almost any major university computing system. Pine was instrumental in establishing the IMAP standard for e-mail agents, which was also developed at the University of Washington. Recently the Pine development team was the recipient of a $100,000 award in recognition of its contribution to resources available to the Internet community. Yet, Pine is generally not a commercial product, though it performs with the quality of one, and has been integrated into commercial products (Pine's license allowed anyone to copy and distribute at no charge but not to distribute modifications without permission—thus ensuring a strong standard). Pine's value has been in the leadership position established by the University of Washington, and the working relationships with the Internet development community. Licensing revenue—even a large amount of it—could not purchase the goodwill and visibility attained by the Pine distribution program.

LABORATORY PROJECT BUDGETS

Of the approximately $39.6 million generated from licensing software and information assets through Digital Ventures since 1990, more than $16.4 million (or about 40 percent) has been returned directly to projects (labs or their equivalent) to bootstrap the University's development efforts. This return to projects is about three times greater than comparable support available through the university's patent program. Funds returned to projects facilitate distribution of research tools directly from labs; support standards; enable the curation, maintenance, and access to databases in a variety of disciplines; and manage internal enterprises in preparation for spinning off as start-up companies. Research groups have created their own Internet portals to connect with the world and distribute their work; some projects are managed by our office while others are identified through our OpenDoor portal, a Digital Ventures program to raise the visibility of software released freely by university software developers.

At the University of Washington, researchers may choose whether to reinvest (a portion or all royalties on an annual basis) or take a personal share as a "dividend" beyond the costs of ongoing development and distribution. Thirty-seven of our eighty active revenue-generating projects are currently reinvesting in their technology transfer activities. This represents half of the licensing revenue as well! This has not dampened entrepreneurship in any way. We have assisted nine start-ups, for instance, in the last three years. If anything, reinvestment and the goodwill associated with referrals to our office have expanded entrepreneurship at the University of Washington by enabling projects to grow internally, with some spinning off at much higher valuations than typical for university technologies.

Administrators must be attuned to the power of project budgets. Revenue support is essential to fuel teaching, research, and retention of talent. We were fortunate to have the flexibility in our practice to provide multiple channels for bringing resources to researchers and their projects. We found that university software developers are sensitive to costs, particularly if they have chosen to reinvest in the research project rather than take a personal share of licensing revenue. Digital Ventures, supported by the vice provost, waived its administrative fee for a number of projects in order to bootstrap the transfer activity and ensure that the immediate needs of the projects were addressed first. In other cases, Digital Ventures worked in concert with development channels to raise gift support for projects rather than rely solely on downstream fees from licensing.

Phrap, Phred, Consed, and Repeatmasker

A suite of bioinformatics software tools—Phrap, Phred, Consed, and Repeatmasker—was created by Professor Phil Green and his lab personnel during the mid-1990s. The algorithms used by the programs were published in the scholarly literature and, fortunately—from the perspective of Digital Ventures—no patent rights were available. The Green laboratory was not interested in "commercialization" but did want the suite to become the "de facto standard" in bioinformatics in part because of the race going on at the time between the public and private human genome sequencing projects. The lab wanted a simple, "painless" distribution to public genome centers and other academics willing to share data under the public project's rules (immediate release of data as it is generated). For those who were following a proprietary path, there was an expectation that a reasonable fee should be paid and that the funds received would help accelerate the public project. When we became involved, the lab had already made the software available to a few companies, with the understanding that if a licensing effort were ever developed, the companies would participate in it.

Digital Ventures worked with the Green laboratory to create distribution programs for academics and for-profit organizations. The lab put a simple statement of expectations for academic users on its Web site and provided code to users when a user confirmed agreement with the lab's statement. We did not make academics sign licenses, or collect signatures of "authorized contracting officers" at receiving organizations. For companies, we wanted adoption to be as broad as possible while generating funding to support ongoing software development, so we adopted a site licensing program for industry, charging a fee of $10,500 for software in the suite, with individual codes available separately for fees ranging from $500 to $5,000. For their payment, recipients received a site license to make as many copies as desired at their site and to modify the software for use at the site. We placed no restrictions on disclosure or reverse engineering, and we did not require modifications to be provided back to the lab. More important, recipients obtained updates to the software made available by the Green lab in the next year with no additional formalities, and gained expedited access to lab personnel for assistance with the science and implementation of the software. Recipients could extend the update and lab service for additional years for 40 percent of the fee originally paid, and with their renewal, they received an option to extend their site license company-wide. If they chose not to pay, they still retained the license to the software they had received. Our goal was to promote use, so it made no sense to ask recipients to stop using the software merely for nonpayment. As long as the software continued to develop and the lab remained interested, recipients were motivated to continue the relationship with the project.

Revenue from the distribution program was managed through a memorandum of understanding with the Green lab, providing for most of the funds to be dedicated back to the lab, with a small portion declared as a "dividend" to be allocated to the university's copyright royalty sharing schedule, and 15 percent retained by Digital Ventures to recognize its contribution to the effort.

As distribution scaled from a few company sites to dozens, we also received inquiries from companies that wanted to distribute the suite or integrate it into their product offerings. In addition to allowing redistribution of our software source, we also licensed a number of companies to distribute executables only with the idea that some companies did not want source code from a university lab but wanted a true software vendor that would support the software as a product. This expanded the reach of our distribution program well beyond our own efforts. After nine years and over $7 million in licensing revenue received, we have developed hundreds of company contacts, distribution arrangements with more than ten companies adding value through their own development work, and have become the de facto standard.

As the distribution project developed, we dealt with a number of challenges. When the primary developer of one of the codes left the university, following our relationship model, we moved distribution and management of that code to the company he joined. One of the codes in the suite was developed with a third-party software tool that changed the terms in its license several years into our distribution. This forced one of the lab's programmers to spend more than a month removing elements of the tool from the code and using a new tool consistent with our licensing program.

By developing hundreds of site licenses with industry contacts, we created what is known as a "channel"—a pattern of repeat business with organizations who know how to work with us. Though channels are well known in marketing, they are not generally considered in patent management. The Phrap channel is an example of a distinct intangible asset created by Digital Ventures—one that has a value independent of the software transactions that created it. Once we had developed the Phrap channel, we were able to use it to inform recipients of the availability of Polyphred, a related software tool developed by another laboratory at the University of Washington. The Phrap channel provided a ready-made distribution program for the Polyphred project.

DRUG INTERACTION DATABASE

The Drug Interaction Database started as a need identified by Professor Rene Levy in the Department of Pharmaceutics. Both industry and government recognized the need to gather published information to identify and anticipate adverse interactions between drugs. The database currently contains in vitro and in vivo information on drug interactions in humans from 5,920 publications referenced in Medline, 16 new drug applications, and 217 product labels. It is updated daily. Access to the database is licensed by Digital Ventures for organizations interested in drug interactions, particularly scientists working in drug discovery and drug development and clinicians who desire in-depth information.

When Digital Ventures started working on this project in 1999, however, there was only a prototype needing a great deal of work. Digital Ventures helped the project obtain nearly $1 million in gifts, typically as two- or three-year commitments in the range of $20,000 from industry to build a first version. We promised to use the money to develop the database and to make the resulting work available to industry and government for a reasonable fee. Digital Ventures created a subscription service, worked to manage relationships with suppliers of technology to the project, and helped the developers of the Drug Interaction Database make the transition from individual efforts to thinking in terms of a project. Subscription revenues in support of the database are now over $600,000 per year, five years into the distribution effort. Critical to the public presentation of the subscription effort is the project's Web site, which makes it clear that the licensing funds are reinvested in supporting the Drug Interaction Database.

NETBOT

In 1994, during the emergence of the World Wide Web, Brian Pinkerton, a graduate student in computer science, created the Webcrawler, the first full-text search engine on the Internet. He fielded the Webcrawler on a university server and Digital Ventures worked with him and the department to secure financial support from a local car dealership (of all things). Soon it was clear that Webcrawler was getting the attention of the investment community and Digital Ventures began receiving inquiries from venture capital firms.

Although the software was fielded on a university server, and Digital Ventures had provided assistance, it was also clear that the software was not owned by the university. As commercial concerns approached Pinkerton, Digital Ventures agreed that it would be important to establish provenance of the software, and so drafted and signed a letter confirming that the university had no ownership interest in the software. This simple willingness to waive a claim to a clearly important new development turned out to be tremendously valuable for everyone concerned. The graduate student was able to make a deal to sell the Webcrawler to America Online, an up-and-coming Web portal company.

The waiver of an interest played an important role in demonstrating to the computer science department that Digital Ventures was committed to the best outcomes, not the most money.

A computer science faculty member approached Digital Ventures with a new search technology substantially more advanced than that of Webcrawler. Digital Ventures developed a distribution project, but before we closed our first site license, we brought in two venture capital firms for interviews, and in 1996, two computer science faculty and their graduate students were able to start Netbot to develop commercial versions of their research technologies, including Metacrawler, the first search agent to use multiple search engines to create a composite search report. The success of Netbot (acquired by Excite in 1997 for $35 million) helped to develop a working relationship between computer science faculty and Digital Ventures. A hallmark of the relationship was that Digital Ventures did not insist on taking ownership of software, did not use a "one-size-fits-all" approach to software distribution, was honest about what it could and could not accomplish, and worked to facilitate the directions that software developers were interested in pursuing. We effectively used this same approach to a succession of start-ups based in computer science, working within formal university processes and helping faculty and graduate students keep their personal work clear of institutional claims.

OPERATING IN THE SHADOW OF PATENTS

Patents are often described as a "stronger" intellectual property right. Certainly patents require substantial resources to secure—the application process easily may cost $10,000. The patent process is open to systemization that is relatively straightforward to state in policy. However, emphasis on patent rights can interfere with actually getting technology and information into the hands of early adopters through copyright strategies. In applying for a patent, a patent office has an immediate problem: how to recover that $10,000 investment? The resolution generally lies in finding a commercialization partner sometime in the ensuing five, ten, or fifteen years. The value of software lies in getting it quickly into the hands of those who can validate the work and develop long-term relationships that will sustain the project and the laboratory's reputation.

There is also the perception that copyright licensing is easier to do or of lower value. In the last six years, copyrights have accounted for more than 90 percent of Digital Ventures' licensing income. This is not because copyright licensing is easier or less valuable. Software licensing, often a hybrid of multiple forms of intellectual property, can be as complex as any patent deal. The great challenge, however, is to find the appropriate register of relationship that the laboratory desires to create with its primary external community of researchers, both in nonprofit and for-profit organizations.

Software intellectual property management will necessarily disrupt processes, policy, and informational materials in a patent-based office. Software management starts with project formation, not disclosure; software doesn't depend on a single form of intellectual property and so is nearly always composite; software developers may contribute in a range of ways—as inventors, programmers, designers, reviewers, and documentation writers—whereas invention management is based on determining the "true inventors," usually with reference to patent law. Working with copyright necessitates earlier involvement with developers than a patent office normally expects. Software management can effectively start before a line of code has been written. When a code has been "finished," it is often too late to sort out the complications that have arisen in development. Distribution may take many forms, most often as nonexclusive licensing, with limited exclusive arrangements riding "on top" for specific applications. Starting from copyrights, we found that intellectual property attaching to software can be split many ways. A common distinction is to divide rights between internal uses (make, use, copy, modify) and external exploitation rights (sell, distribute, import, sublicense). Focusing first on internal applications and uses has been fundamental to Digital Ventures. If there is an active user community, then many other good things may happen, including commercial product development.

These differences led the University of Washington to establish Digital Ventures as a separate intellectual property unit in 1997. This was an inspired decision, reducing tension with the patent licensing office and giving the software practice operating freedom. While the Digital Ventures unit does pursue patents where appropriate (our current patent budget is $250,000 and is focused on start-up opportunities), the key to our practice is early contact and partnering with faculty and students to position informatics assets as an extension of teaching and research. There is nothing gained in the efficiency argument that all intellectual property should be managed through one set of policies or processes. Quite the contrary, attempting to treat copyright as "patent" spelled funny may damage the overall technology transfer program, creating useless red tape and ill will for the sake of consistency and administrative convenience. At an abstract level "intellectual property" has some common attributes—it arises with new developments, it may be owned, assigned, and licensed, and it may exclude others from exploiting assets—but beyond this, there are great differences. Software and copyright drive deep into the heart of research, instruction, and administration. The typical policies and practices of a patent-based office are not suited to software and copyright practice. The opportunities to advance university goals as expressed at the level of software developed in laboratories, projects, and collaborations far exceed the convenience of having a single operating model for "intellectual property."

Relationship-Based Intellectual Property Management

Developing relationship-based technology transfer is a long-term investment. A software licensing project typically takes several years to mature as the software asset is validated through peer review; distribution of the software to early adopters creates an audience; eventually, broader interest (and revenue support) from industry follows. One must have the discipline to create reasonable expectations and not to undertake more projects than the office can manage well. As many technology transfer offices can attest, reputation is crucial and recovery from missteps with faculty is long and painful. Our practice grew from referral rather than broadcast advertisement, and we worked to understand each research project's goals so that we could provide meaningful choices of transfer models to support those goals.

Research groups rarely give much thought to distribution and possible commercial uses of their work. We participate in conversations on strategy and outcomes which can run months (sometimes years!) as busy software developers try to fit one more thing into their schedules. To be effective, we had to become a reliable source of expertise, and candid about those things we simply did not know. Digital Ventures hired professionals with strong business development skills who did not oversell and had a passion for and an understanding of university research and the points of pain experienced by faculty and students. We also worked to develop and retain our personnel to foster and maintain relationships with researchers, departments, and schools. One of the clear messages we received from faculty was that changing case managers multiple times during a project was not acceptable. We make a concerted effort to ensure continuity in the Digital Ventures unit so that researchers are partnered with at least two case managers (a lead and a "wing"). Doing so provides continuity in the relationship if the lead manager leaves and also increases our productivity, efficiency, and support for our partnering researcher's vision.

INTELLECTUAL PROPERTY POLICIES

University intellectual property policies are often the product of committee drafting and numerous compromises that can threaten informatics and relationship-based technology transfer models (primarily the incentives for faculty and student participation when there are other alternatives available). No policy can improve on good decision making by department chairs, deans, and the technology transfer office. We were fortunate to start with a copyright policy with sufficient inconsistency and generality to allow an effective software practice to evolve and change in response to environmental conditions. An absolutist, one-size-fits-all policy would have killed our program before it got off the ground.

Recent changes in the University of Washington intellectual property policy threaten our ability to reinvest directly in research projects, demonstrating how even successful programs may be fundamentally misunderstood. Several of our key portfolios got off the ground because Digital Ventures waived its administrative fee until the project approached sustainability. Licensing revenue in FY2006 was $4.1 million for the Digital Ventures unit, and the expectation is that our administrative fee recovered from licensing revenue should cover the $800,000 budget of the unit. Researchers reinvesting in technology transfer activities rather than taking a personal share find it hard to accept a high administrative fee, even though they value the work that we do. In 2003, administration officials created an unfortunate debate over ownership of software, which had the potential to interfere with Digital Venture's working relationship with faculty and students. It took significant effort for Digital Ventures to retain a stewardship model over copyrighted works, data, and other informatics assets. Ownership of software by the university alone will seldom provide opportunity because a diverse set of intangible assets—including the developers' expertise—will need to be aggregated in order to reach practical application, let alone downstream commercial product development, and this requires significant cooperation between the developers and Digital Ventures. In sixteen years, Digital Ventures has not experienced a positive outcome where ownership demands trumped partnership. University leaders should challenge efforts to "harmonize" patent and copyright policies by making all intellectual property appear to follow a single operating model. In the case of software, patent-based models in particular are often inappropriate and painfully ineffective.

If one were to establish anew a general intellectual property program for a university, we suggest basing it on software and other forms of scholarly communication, reserving patent-based commercial licensing as a subspecialty with limited application. Beyond all, trademark—goodwill, reputation, "brand"—is the most important form of intellectual property a university can manage. A policy that linked scholarly communication with goodwill and reputation would go a long way toward providing the operating guidance necessary to handle copyright and patent matters.

One can aim to make $20 million in licensing per year by getting a 2 percent running royalty on a big-hit patent deal with a monster product generating $1 billion per year in sales. Or one can follow the approach of Digital Ventures, and aim to use various forms of intellectual property to establish fifty projects, each with eighty or so industry relationships, each relationship producing on the order of $5,000 per year. Both approaches are long-term propositions. Both are challenging goals to achieve. The difference is that creating that big hit may take a decade in top university patent licensing programs, whereas software distribution programs may progressively build a substantial network of external collaborators more valuable than the transactions that establish it. In the end, the big hit agreement runs its course as a single, albeit tremendously important, relationship, but with the project-based approach, the university has developed thousands of relationships and has access to a wide range of companies, research sites, and expertise. A software unit employing this approach becomes a crucial tool in expanding the reach of the university, emphasizing small but important transactions rather than a sequence of failed efforts justified once a decade by a big hit. There are some great patent licensing shops in university practice. They would be even greater if they were complemented by robust support for a spectrum of software dissemination models.

Closing Thoughts

To develop a software-based management unit, it is crucial to separate software intellectual property from conventional patent management processes. Allow distribution income to be returned to the project, and take a "dividend" only when project costs are properly recovered and the developers elect to receive personally a share of the income. Encourage open source distributions in order to build relationships and reputation. Develop policy that permits intellectual property professionals to use their best judgment and that offers a range of contracting tools to provide each project with the resources that meet the goals and register of engagement suited to its interests. At its heart, technology transfer is instruction that enables, permits, and supports. Encourage the transfer function to be located as close to the laboratory or development unit as possible. Offer choices to software developers and manage the software intellectual property office as if involvement with software developers is a privilege rather than a requirement forced by an ownership policy. Learn from experience and incorporate new models into established practice. The most important thing is the ability to mobilize intellectual property for a public purpose. The metrics of success for software transfer are the relationships formed, the leadership positions established, and the resources flowing to the development enterprise. Digital Ventures at the

University of Washington has been a leader in demonstrating the benefits of this approach.

Can this approach to technology transfer extend beyond software? We believe so. Inventions shorn of their patent armor are also fundamentally new information assets, capable of being taught to companies. Method-based inventions share a great deal in common with software. Software is not much more than a particular implementation of methods to accomplish a purpose. Though method patents may be used to protect investments in manufacturing processes and equipment, in a wide range of situations, including disease assays and business operations, it makes sense for universities to adopt approaches pioneered by software developers.

Research consortia, similarly, are designed around a nonexclusive approach to licensing. Consortia emphasize long-term relationships and collaboration, and can be the source of substantial, sustained research funding. A nonexclusive software distribution program with a laboratory budget operates in the same fashion as a membership-based consortium, but receives its funding through a license relationship rather than by gift or sponsored research contract. There are advantages to the software transfer approach. "Membership" is based on actual use of research assets rather than on a presumption that in the future something might be developed of value. The laboratory has the freedom of gift funding to pursue its own vision, and the flexibility of royalty management to share benefits with its innovators and with supporting administrative units. The cost of membership in a software distribution–based consortium may be much lower than the conventional consortium, which may require a commitment of $30,000 or more per year. A low fee allows the distribution program to scale readily and enables small and mid-sized companies to participate—a class of companies largely ignored by conventionally sponsored research and licensing programs.

This approach to software management also points to university involvement in the development of interoperable systems, platforms, and standards—all important to industry and virtually absent from patent licensing office annual reports. Standards licensing involves making technology available nonexclusively on reasonable and non-discriminatory terms. In addition to establishing a leadership position for the university, standards also may be the source of significant revenue through licensing income, as well as through follow-on sponsored research. Patent administration at universities is under attack from some industries in part because universities are unwilling to release inventions to be used in precompetitive industry development environments, even when doing so would result in widespread adoption of new technology, encourage entrepreneurship, and build goodwill. One reason universities do not do this is that their patent policies assume that each patent case must earn royalties to recover the costs of obtaining patents and to be shared with inventors. Once the decision is made to seek a patent, a university licensing office is all but "locked in" to trying to find a paying licensee. Software management teaches that such "lock in" need not dominate invention management.

If one were to start with an *innovation* policy for a university rather than patent and copyright policies, one would develop an office to facilitate the movement of information assets through collaboration, entrepreneurship, and investment to practical application. Part lending library, part agricultural extension, part medical clinic—an innovation office would focus on encouraging important adopting audiences to use distinctive research findings. With an innovation policy, we would be reminded that technology transfer is fundamentally instruction, with delivery, permissions, assurances, and follow-on assistance to enable independent practice of new technology. Publication and conference presentations get at only part of an innovation policy's objectives, by announcing findings. Licensing alone merely promises not to sue—an ironic position for universities to take, by any account. An innovation policy would focus talent and resources on connecting academic leaders with industry scientists, entrepreneurs, and investors through inclusive contracts rather than exclusionary positions. The software transfer experience at the University of Washington's Digital Ventures makes evident the possibilities of focusing on inclusive, scalable, extensible relationships to grow the research enterprise.

ACKNOWLEDGMENTS

The authors acknowledge their colleagues both academic and professional who have contributed much of the intellectual thought, built the systems, and managed the projects that drive Digital Ventures. Dr. Patrick Jones and Ms. Dana Bostrom deserve special notice for their efforts to advance software transfer practice and philosophy, and we maintain an active collaboration although we are now at different institutions. Numerous graduate students researched and built Digital Ventures' systems and a series of contract managers created the office environment necessary to succeed in a relationship-based activity.

CHAPTER FIVE

CONSORTIA IMPLEMENTATIONS AND TECHNOLOGY TRANSFER

P. L. Jones

This chapter addresses key aspects in the development, management, and operation of university-industry consortia derived from experience gained through the Center for Process Analytical Chemistry (CPAC) at the University of Washington (www.cpac.washington.edu/). CPAC was established in 1984 as a National Science Foundation Industry/University Cooperative Research Center (I/UCRC); it is now a self-sustaining center funded by its industry partners and educational activities. It is one of the longest-standing centers of its kind with over thirty members and an annual budget in excess of $1,000,000. I address lessons learned about the pros and cons of university-industry consortia as a means of promoting university-industry relations.

OVERVIEW

University-industry consortia refer to a set of companies and one or multiple universities that agree to pursue collaborative research dedicated to a particular problem, theme, or discipline. Consortia are frequently the best arrangement for developing a particular area of broad research, defining relevant problems and deploying techniques and information to the private sector. The base terms for intellectual property management are usually nonexclusive, which ensures the most inclusive deployment possible. If properly structured, the deployment may be broad and effective.

In their best incarnations, university-industry consortia create a rich research environment with many partners sharing information and facilities. Support for research effort takes many forms: funding research through philanthropy to the university, gifting to specific research groups, directly sponsored research, annual fees, exchange of personnel, collaborative interactions without funding, specialized education and, in some instances, follow-on funding of specific projects by a subset of the participants. Mixed in with these support-based interactions are those such as the exchange of personnel, either as visiting scientists or interns, collaborative interactions without funding, and specialized education. Typically, a university-industry consortium involves, either directly or indirectly, many if not all of these elements. Consortia also present, however, a challenging framework for structuring administrative tasks and managing relationships among diverse participants.

Researchers, academic administrators, and corporate R&D managers contemplating a new consortium have a range of structuring options and associated decisions to consider. Choices that anticipate growth in relationships and opportunities increase the longevity and stability of the consortium but can come at the cost of complicating the resulting sponsorship agreements and their implementation. By envisioning the effort too narrowly, partners may fail to include broad considerations that increase the value to each party, such as how one recruits new senior or junior faculty participants or how to enlist a researcher from another university to meet a specific research need. Conversely, trying to cover all possibilities for relations without concrete need often causes the effort to fail through unnecessary complexity.

Consortia are easier to establish if motivated by leveraged funding. The central sponsor during the formative period is especially important. Its presence and resources lend validation to the concept and make it easier to bring in members. The National Science Foundation (NSF) has been central in establishing and promoting this model. Over the last two decades, NSF has sponsored the formation of consortia through the Industry-University

Cooperative Research Center (I/UCRC), the Engineering Research Center and the Science and Technology Center programs (www.nsf.gov/eng/iip/iucrc/directory/overview.jsp). This has led to a new era of partnerships between universities and industry. Consortia that are initiated with NSF funding, however, must eventually make the transition to being self-sustaining through direct support from industry partners and other activities. Self-sustainability is expected in five to ten years after initial funding. Other activities might include contributions or grants, industry-targeted professional development courses and summer courses, professional services, expanded membership, and facilities use charges.

ADVANTAGES ASSOCIATED WITH CONSORTIA

The value of a consortium to a university and to its external participants can be grouped into five categories (see Table 5.1). The elements in each category are varied and do not necessarily link across categories. The emphasis here is on the value to industrial participants; the points below can be viewed as selling points or the value proposition for participation; there are complementary values to the university.

1. **Peer communication.** A neutral forum is provided for networking and facilitating sponsor-to-center and sponsor-to-sponsor interaction. The networking serves as an information clearinghouse and subject matter resource center, a location for semiannual sponsor meetings, and a forum for benchmarking. Peer-facilitated focus groups may define common current industry cluster research needs.

2. **New knowledge generation.** Innovation is optimized by: (a) leveraged funding and combined resources; (b) access to scientists, research facilities, and increased awareness of broad ongoing research; (c) sponsor input for new proposal selection for base technology development; (d) sponsor-directed special projects on base technology (R&D for sponsors); and (e) teaming opportunities.

TABLE 5.1. SUMMARY OF BENEFITS IN A UNIVERSITY-INDUSTRY CONSORTIUM

Peer Communication	New Knowledge Generation	Highly Qualified Personnel	Continuing Education	Research Tools and Artifacts
Networking: sponsor-to-center and sponsor-to-sponsor interaction	Leveraged funding and combined resources	Area-specific postdoctoral fellowships	Short courses and seminars	Publications and theses
Information clearinghouse and subject matter resource center	Access to scientists, research facilities, and increased awareness of broad ongoing research	Area-specific student support through stipends to student	On-site customized training opportunities	Progress reports for current research, test data, and protocols
Peer-facilitated focus groups defining common current industry cluster research needs	Sponsor input for new proposal selection for base technology development	Cooperative opportunities in sponsor companies	Visiting scientist program	Software, devices, and prototypes
Benchmarking	Sponsor directed special projects on base technology (R&D for sponsors)	Input into interdisciplinary curriculum development	In-depth summer programs	Testing and specialized services
Semiannual sponsor meetings	Teaming opportunities	Recruiting advantages	Consultation	Intellectual property rights access and internal use

3. **Qualified personnel.** The context supports the development of highly qualified personnel with increased knowledge of participant needs and cultures. These benefits may include: (a) area-specific postdoctoral fellowships; (b) area-specific student support through stipends; (c) cooperative opportunities in sponsor companies; (d) input into interdisciplinary curriculum development; and (e) recruiting advantages.

4. **Continuing education.** Need-specific and customized continuing education for corporate personnel is valuable and desirable and may include: (a) short courses and seminars; (b) on-site customized training opportunities; (c) visiting scientist programs; (d) in-depth summer programs; and (e) consultation.

5. **Research tools and artifacts.** Early access to research tools and artifacts is vital and comes in various forms: (a) publications and theses; (b) progress reports for current research, test data, and protocols; (c) software, devices, and prototypes; (d) testing and specialized services; and (e) intellectual property right access and internal use.

As in many university-industry settings, the value of the interaction to the participants may extend far beyond simple involvement in a research project. Planners that consider and emphasize this broader value in putting the consortium agreement in place can positively influence the negotiations over the more controversial elements of a consortium agreement, such as access to intellectual property rights.

OPERATING PHILOSOPHY

Sponsorship agreements set the baseline for the operating philosophy of a center and the establishment of the group norms that define the interactions among the participants. Typically these agreements focus on two primary topics: the organization of the center and the disposition of intellectual property rights arising under center funding. With respect to organization, the focus of the technology transfer within a university-industry consortium is often used to help set up the structure and expectations for relationships between the sponsors and the university as well as among the sponsors themselves. This is particularly important regarding intellectual property rights among sponsors. At CPAC the sponsorship agreement had to be revised after eight years to restructure intellectual property handling and then again after fifteen years to deal with the transition to independence from being an NSF center, and to include associate members.

Knowledge Transfer to All Participants

A major task of a university in managing the consortium is to coordinate knowledge transfer activities among the groups and institutions involved. One must ensure that the sponsorship agreement reflects the desired technology transfer outcomes and that it is compatible with the various activities of participating research groups. The sponsorship agreement must also properly reflect the policies and aims of the center and the institution. In a university environment the typical research group interacts with diverse faculty and other research units, runs multiple projects across an array of interests, and funds its activities from numerous sources. The creation of information assets and intellectual property occurs over time and under sponsorship from a large variety of sources via grants from, or contracts with, federal and nonfederal external entities. These funding patterns define the landscape in which knowledge within a center is created and where the accompanying technology transfer takes place. To illustrate the complexities of this environment, the flow of a technology development involving the creation of one of the licensed CPAC technologies is presented below along with the agreements that affected the process (see Figure 5.1).

Within CPAC, there was sufficient flexibility and experience to enable rather than disable the participation of multiple parties as well as to encourage a project that involved several nonmembers, a substantial Department of Energy grant, and licensing to a small business outside of the member group that worked with the sponsorship to deploy the results.

Basic Management Structure

The basic structure for many industrial consortia, whether at a single site or replicated across multiple sites, typically involves

Figure 5.1. A Flow Diagram Showing the Complexities of Consortium
Technology Creation

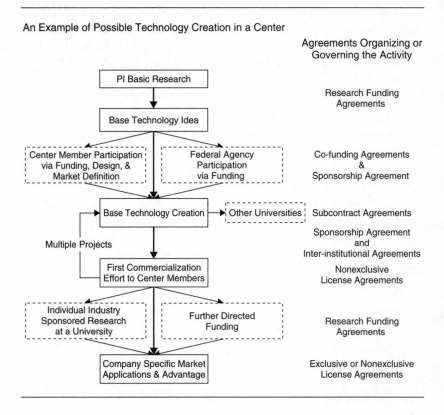

An Example of Possible Technology Creation in a Center

Agreements Organizing or
Governing the Activity

PI Basic Research

Research Funding
Agreements

Base Technology Idea

Center Member Participation via Funding, Design, & Market Definition

Federal Agency Participation via Funding

Co-funding Agreements
&
Sponsorship Agreement

Base Technology Creation

Other Universities

Subcontract Agreements

Multiple Projects

Sponsorship Agreement
and
Inter-institutional Agreements

First Commercialization Effort to Center Members

Nonexclusive
License Agreements

Individual Industry Sponsored Research at a University

Further Directed Funding

Research Funding
Agreements

Company Specific Market Applications & Advantage

Exclusive or Nonexclusive
License Agreements

a local administrative director managing day-to-day center activities, a faculty director managing academic and research programs, a governing policy committee or board (predominantly from the university) setting overall policy for operations and oversight, and an industrial advisory board (IAB) representing the combined interests of the outside members and composed of one voting member from each sponsor. In many centers and consortia, the administrative and faculty director are the same individual. In CPAC these are set up as separate positions so that the sponsors have a direct point of contact with a focus only on CPAC activities, and the university has someone focused on delivery of programs, sponsors, and faculty recruitment and sponsor retention. The head of the policy committee is the vice provost for research and the chair of the IAB is elected by the IAB. For convenience, administrative functions such as staff appointments, accounting, and so forth are set up through one department, usually that of the faculty director.

In addition to the main management elements outlined above, CPAC utilizes an IAB steering committee appointed by the chair of the IAB, which is intended to help ensure that the research direction of the center is aligned with the goals and problems of the industrial members. This group meets several times per year, reviews and solicits proposals to provide feedback to the faculty, coordinates collaborative projects (for example, field testing of prototypes with the sponsors), and helps the administrative and faculty directors prioritize funding opportunities for presentation to the full IAB. Recently, this structure was supplemented with an IAB executive committee—consisting of the past, current, and incoming IAB chairs—that represents the IAB in policy or other discussions with the university. The organizational structure of CPAC is shown in Figure 5.2.

FIGURE 5.2.   CPAC ORGANIZATIONAL STRUCTURE

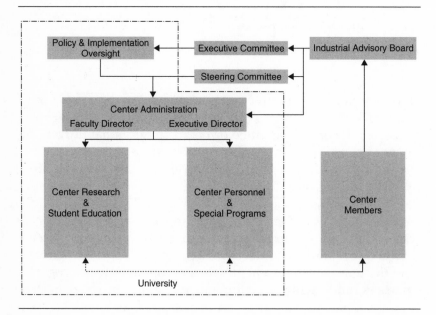

CONSORTIA WITH MULTIPLE UNIVERSITIES

In constructing a university-industry consortium involving multiple universities, two basic approaches exist. One is to place all the universities on an essentially equal footing with an overarching coordinating agreement among the universities and a common sponsorship agreement. The second is to have one university be the prime contractor and engage other universities as subcontractors whether or not they are ongoing members of the consortium. The first approach, the most common one, enables each university to be equal, but at the expense of complicating teaming and building strong relations among the sponsors and the universities. The second, a standard university contracting approach, simplifies the management of sponsor relations and integrates the projects across a broader spectrum, although at the expense of more effective local interactions. It also has the advantage of flexibility and simplicity for the sponsors and the universities because it reduces interactions to simple binary interactions of standard form. The two approaches are illustrated in Figure 5.3.

FIGURE 5.3. ALTERNATIVES IN MULTI-UNIVERSITY CONSORTIA

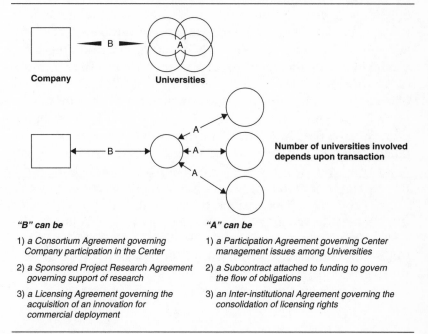

"B" can be

1) a Consortium Agreement governing Company participation in the Center

2) a Sponsored Project Research Agreement governing support of research

3) a Licensing Agreement governing the acquisition of an innovation for commercial deployment

"A" can be

1) a Participation Agreement governing Center management issues among Universities

2) a Subcontract attached to funding to govern the flow of obligations

3) an Inter-institutional Agreement governing the consolidation of licensing rights

After the first ten years of funding from NSF, CPAC faced the issue of how to broaden its research base to other universities if it wished to receive additional funding from NSF. In addition, the corporate sponsors were interested in accessing complementary research expertise in the focus areas of the consortium. CPAC, in consultation with the policy board, and at the strong urging of the IAB, chose to use the second approach mentioned above. From a technology management perspective this has proved a simple approach to manage through standard inter-institutional agreements.

Managing Intellectual Property

In response to concerns of members, CPAC revised the sponsorship agreement with regard to the management of intellectual property rights. This change was prompted by several factors:

1. When critical decisions needed to be made, arising center technologies were inevitably in early stages of development due to the center's open environment, and therefore were riskier to develop than was common in the industry or preferable to members. This made it difficult to obtain a consensus among members to fund patents that would be needed to advance technology adoption later. To overcome this obstacle, decisions regarding protection of intellectual property were moved to the University of Washington's Office of Technology Transfer. This had the effect of balancing control of decision making with the motivation to make decisions wisely. This mode of control was possible, in part, because the University of Washington maintained an ample patent fund, but the results indicate that even universities with fewer resources should consider utilizing this approach, provided the use rights of members are similar to those described below.

2. Contrary to expectations, broad intellectual property rights to members decreased rather than increased the likelihood that innovations from research were deployed. Although members utilized the knowledge arising from the research, being the first to invest in new technology platforms was unattractive. Most members preferred to adopt a "wait-and-see" strategy.

3. Rights adoption that required members to opt out of opportunities rather than opt in blocked deployment of innovations because there was a perceived risk of placing another party in a potentially superior competitive position. This meant, for example, that members would not agree to grant an exclusive license to a potential competitor, such as a start-up company, even if they had no interest in the technology.

4. It was critical to clarify time lines and trigger points for acquiring and losing intellectual property rights. Consequently, use rights were redefined as being granted only to those who were members of the consortium on the day the disclosure for patentable and copyrightable matter was received by the University's Office of Technology Transfer.

During the establishment of a consortium, members find that their base rights are one of the most contentious issues. A mistake made in the structure of the original CPAC agreement was to lump all types of intellectual property together under one definition. This reduced the clarity of what internal use rights meant for nonpatented research artifacts and information as well as hindered actual management and delivery of the promised rights. The CPAC agreement granted each member a restricted set of nonexclusive use rights to intellectual property disclosed during their membership with a time-limited option to license further rights. These "internal use" rights allowed the sponsors and their affiliates to do the following:

- Make, use, have made, and import patented subject matter
- Reproduce and make derivatives of copyrightable materials provided through projects as well as to use, perform, display, and transmit the same within its sites
- Use technical information created through center research for any purpose subordinate to the grants associated with patents and copyrights and subject to the confidentiality provisions of the sponsorship agreement

Access to prototypes and research materials was under standard material transfer agreements.

CORPORATE CONCERNS WITH THE AGREEMENT

Member companies express a set of concerns during formation of consortia:

1. *Extent of rights.* Internal use rights expressly did not include the rights to sell, offer to sell, or sublicense patented subject matter or to redistribute, perform, or display copyrightable material for the benefit of others.

2. *Rights of affiliates.* Affiliates were defined as entities owned or controlled by sponsors with at least 49 percent ownership, where the ownership stake accounted for affiliates in countries where majority ownership was not allowed. Parent companies were not affiliates, and internal use rights and information were not transferable from the subsidiaries to parent companies.

3. *Relative competitive advantage gained by membership.* This concern centered on the value proposition discussed earlier vis-a-vis the rights to exploit IP at will.

4. *Cost for use of IP arising from sponsorship.* This concern is common to all industry-sponsored research. Corporations fear "exorbitant license fees" for unfettered use of IP subsequent to "paying for the research," in this case through their membership fees. This is the common misperception of "paying twice" for the use of results because of the requirement to license rights beyond internal use rights after having sponsored the research in the first place.

After eight years of operation, the established relationships within CPAC led to a sound understanding of these concerns. The R&D managers came to an understanding that proved seminal. Intellectual property rights wanted in a university-industry interaction, and actually achieved in the first sponsorship agreement, ran counter to their long-term interests. That is, access to rights did not lead automatically to development of innovation. A corollary was that although many ideas explored by CPAC were promising and applications downstream could be envisioned, the realities of their product development meant that the R&D managers needed to focus their own development efforts elsewhere. In a sense, companies had the rights but no one was willing to run the risks associated with the development of center ideas to a usable platform—except in those rare advances that would be unambiguously successful and applicable to currently defined needs, none of which occurred in those first eight years. This outcome also ran counter to the role of the university as a promoter of knowledge adoption.

The issue of competitive advantage was addressed by considering not only the time value of information but the broader value elements as well. For example, a large fraction of CPAC graduate students and postdoctorates (at one time more than 85 percent) went to work for members after completing their work at CPAC. The issues of reasonableness and decision making in licensing were taken up by structuring a small dispute resolution committee composed of the vice provost of research, the chair of the industrial advisory board, and another university member selected by mutual agreement. This mechanism has never been invoked or required.

The key issue of licensing for any access beyond a base level was to achieve a balance between legitimate needs on all sides. As noted earlier, rights that were too broad actually undermined what everyone wished to achieve. With respect to paying twice, the underlying assumption is that one paid sufficiently when sponsoring the research even with overhead—that is, a market price was paid rather than a subsidized cost. Even in the best of circumstances corporate sponsors underappreciated the actual subsidies to the research by or through the sponsoring university as well as the difficulty of creating self-sustaining efforts. The federal facilities and administrative (F&A) rate charged by universities is approximately one-half the true F&A required to put facilities at the disposal of the researchers. The difference is made up from other sources including endowments, state or community support of facilities, or university budget lines paid by other sources. Also, graduate student subsidies, which may be from one-third to two-thirds of the rate charged to a project, donated faculty time, and waived use charges increased the leverage that sponsors achieved. This is in addition to the fact that base salary rates for all personnel within a university typically are lower than comparable industrial positions and, therefore, make fundamental research in the university consortium mode cost effective. Furthermore, the interest in centers and single industry-sponsored projects typically arises from a base of activity and resources built over many years from other state and federal sources and, unlike a single-sponsor agreement, multisponsor agreements lower the individual monetary contribution by each member considerably and thus increase the leverage even more. In this context, appropriate licensing may be viewed as delayed payment, a shared risk return to the university above the subsidized cost charged to a sponsor specially positioned to benefit from the work done.

The university did not waive the federal F&A rate attaching to CPAC research efforts but provided extra resources to the center and its projects through the chemistry department, including waiving charges for instrument and electronic shop usage for CPAC research projects.

The combined circumstances and shared experience included the compromise that allowed internal use rights for using technologies toward commercial purposes so long as those uses were compatible with the grants as defined. Thus, use of a device or software internally to improve process control was an internal use. Selling that device or bundling the software with a device to be sold was not. Though such a rights structure seemed to put the instrumentation companies in CPAC at a disadvantage, the broader elements of the value proposition offset considerably the item-specific disadvantage. CPAC was a valuable resource for the instrument companies, enabling them to do market research and test new applications through exceptional access to R&D managers in target companies.

IMPLEMENTATION ALTERNATIVES

Experience in managing CPAC has provided insights into the optimization of various administrative procedures. The following questions should be considered during the establishment of a consortium:

1. Should one allow associate or affiliate members to pay less in sponsorship fees and receive a restricted set of rights or none at all? This is frequently a request of start-up companies. Admitting associate members broadens the membership and helps prospective members to build experience with the center for recruitment

purposes, although it reduces resources and commitment to the center from these entities. Members paying full fees may question the value of full membership or may be reluctant to approve associate members that appear to dilute their benefits. One way the downside can be ameliorated is by limiting the time any company may be an associate member.

2. How does the consortium continue to broaden faculty involvement? Aside from the initial participants, how does a center entice junior faculty to participate or recruit faculty from other institutions? Many times existing participants are reluctant to expand, especially when resources are considered tight. The complexity of being part of a center, the associated obligations of the sponsorship agreement, and the relatively small amounts available to new projects may discourage new participants from investing the time and effort required to become involved.

3. Related to the above, in what manner does the university distribute F&A (overhead) dollars among the departments and colleges? Departments and colleges not receiving support from the indirect funds are reluctant to encourage faculty to participate. A means to address this problem and the above issue is to allow some consortium funding to flow into departments or pilot activities outside the requirements of the consortium agreement. For example, consortium funds can be used at modest levels to augment start-up packages for recruiting new faculty in areas of interest to the IAB without incurring the IP obligations of the sponsorship agreement.

4. Are existing members or nonmembers allowed to help drive a specific project by providing additional funding? This raises the issue of so-called "follow-on or concurrent funding" and its corresponding relationship and IP management issues. The concept of follow-on funding was usually accepted as long as the project was in the open and general summaries of the results were provided to the membership at the semiannual meetings. The key to effective concurrent funding management was to create clear statements separating work on the funded project and work on the center project, and then having both considered by the IAB as they weighed the merits of all center projects. Such balancing is not an easy proposition in the context of broad nonexclusive rights to sponsors from all center-sponsored projects.

One lesson from the experience of CPAC is the importance of structures that promote adoption patterns across the broad range of research groups and among peers in different organizations. In structuring some of the follow-on licensing of CPAC technologies, the university and a few key sponsors worked together to define a nonexclusive license that allowed research managers to bring in technologies on a full commercial basis for a three-year period with minimal cost; consideration in following years would be designed to promote diligence as well as fairness to both sides. This enabled company R&D groups to explore the technology fit for future company applications with assurance that rights were available. Because a cost was associated with the acquisition, it promoted sound decision making in acquiring the rights.

FUTURE CONSORTIA

Traditional consortia are an effective means of establishing research commons involving multiple industrial sponsors. Alternative pathways may also be useful. One promising approach is a technology access program that creates a subscription-based licensing program for a federally funded research project seeking company involvement and validation but with no direct funding for the research. These programs clarify access to research results and intellectual property while simultaneously addressing the costs associated with assembling and distributing information assets, research artifacts, and tools to organizations interested in education through the university and the research group's efforts in technology transfer. Chapter 4 by Charles Williams and Gerald Barnett explores this theme in greater detail.

In designing future collaborative university-industry efforts, experience with CPAC suggests one consider the following.

- For long-term success, build centers around research
  themes that (a) combine several disciplines in an area focusing
  on problems addressing the three-to-five-year time scale
  and bridging the long-term outlook of university research and
  the short-term focus of industrial partners; and (b) support the
  involvement of companies from all points along a market supply
  and distribution chain, preferably across industrial sectors.

- Construct management principles that favor simplicity over the long term with management structures that (a) utilize common university patterns of agreement management in a series of two-party formats, such as prime contractor and subcontractor arrangements for multi-university centers or inter-institutional agreements for intellectual property; and (b) separate center operation management from faculty management of research.
- Choose intellectual property approaches that balance individual and group needs with arrangements that (a) grant a defined set of commercial internal use rights, balancing use with flexibility in promoting availability through licensing within or outside of the membership; (b) set decision making on licensing as an opt-in rather than an opt-out basis; and (c) balance university decision making with the cost of carrying patents.

CHAPTER SIX

ONE-STOP SHOP

Angus Livingstone

This chapter describes the one-stop shop approach of an integrated office that sees its role broadly as industry liaison. It is based on twenty years of experience gained at the University of British Columbia University-Industry Liaison Office. A one-stop shop requires a coordinated approach that addresses the often divergent needs of industry and university researchers. Developing the necessary relationships is an ongoing process. Creating the environment that encourages staff to work together across modalities is vital.

Knowledge transfer between academia and industry is achieved through a multitude of interdependent mechanisms, including graduation of students, publication of manuscripts, conference presentations, offering of student project labs, co-op and intern placements, conducting collaborative research projects, faculty consulting, technology licensing, and spin-off company creation. Some consider the flow of knowledge as being primarily unidirectional—from academia to industry—but in reality the flow is bidirectional. Industry partners provide access to their problems, staff, facilities, and data, all of which enhance and facilitate academic research. Supporting this multiplicity of activities in a coordinated manner in one office encourages synergy among the activities and the efficient use of resources that enhances the effectiveness of the office. Thus, a one-stop shop provides benefits to both industry and faculty.

Industry is better served because the university is in reality a diverse assortment of noncommunicative, dispersed entities (principal investigators, research projects, and laboratories). Moreover, the sales efforts of laboratories vary enormously. Each professor is concerned primarily with his own lab. The faculty is better served by knowledgeable staff that can identify and facilitate collaboration between faculty and relevant local industries, most of which may have distinctive operating procedures. The well-integrated office provides a needed service to both parties and in so doing facilitates university-industry relationships and redounds to the benefit of the community and the state.

The aim of this chapter is to present the concept of a one-stop shop that provides an integrated suite of services and support for both academic researchers and industry. This includes identifying the range of benefits to the institution, their faculty, and industry; considering some of the options when establishing a one-stop shop approach to manage the interaction between industry and universities; and recommending the key issues for consideration by senior university administration.

ONE-STOP SERVICE TO ALL

Companies interfacing with a university often view the institution as a single coordinated entity, much like a corporation with a single CEO firmly in command. In reality, universities normally operate as a community of scholars with minimal coordination between different laboratories or research units. This can leave companies confused and frustrated as with each interaction they endeavor to identify the appropriate university contact and educate him on their company's specific objectives.

The concept of one-stop shopping is therefore highly attractive to companies. It simplifies and accelerates access to the institution's resources by facilitating a deeper understanding of the industry partner's business, operating environment, capabilities and needs, all of which can result in a stronger relationship between the university and its industrial collaborator. It is not intended to be a centralized gatekeeper, but rather the primary point of entry into an organization rich with multiple points of contact.

The concept of one-stop shopping in a university setting, however, can be challenging to grasp, given the diversity and complexity of the environment. This complexity can be categorized in four dimensions: sector (life science, physical science, information technology, and social science); education (project labs, co-op placements, internships, and continuing education programs); research (publications, conference presentations and workshops, research data and tools, and sponsored and collaborative research projects); and geographic (the separation of multiple campus locations or across a university and its affiliated teaching hospitals). Variation along and between dimensions often results in a plethora of different units on the average campus. Each is responsive to the needs of its academic directors, but the units are rarely operated in a coordinated fashion and are often underresourced. This is not the best way to engage industry or optimize the benefits that flow from such engagement.

The benefits of effective engagement of industry and associated knowledge transfer accrue to the students and faculty, the institution, the regional community, and society. Recording and communicating these benefits highlights the university's value and impact in its community, and a one-stop shop is often more effective in gathering and distributing this information. These benefits can be categorized into five separate groups: academic, economic, social, financial, and political.

Academic benefits are manifested through increased access to ongoing support for research at the project level. This includes direct financial support as well as indirect support, such as access to company data, tools, facilities, personnel, and vexing problems. In many disciplines, the opportunity to validate laboratory findings is facilitated through access to the corporate environment. A strong program of university-industry collaboration can also improve a university's effectiveness in recruiting top faculty and graduate students.

Economic benefits to society accrue to the region through the creation of new industries, jobs (particularly for university graduates), investment opportunities, increased productivity through the adoption of new processes and new products, and an expanded tax base. Most economic benefits are realized in the region immediately surrounding the university.

Social benefits flow from the use of new products, processes, and services that promote improved human health, reduced environmental impact, and improved human sustainability. Products include new medical therapies, devices, and vaccines; processes include those for energy production and technologies that can be used to reduce pollutants or remediate contaminated sites.

Financial benefits to the university include the recovery of indirect costs, subsidized or free access to company facilities, vendor discounts, leveraged government funds, royalties, equity, and philanthropy. Companies also benefit financially through maximizing leverage of government funds.

Political benefits include a vibrant local economy, and from that national and international recognition, increased prestige, and industry influence which helps garner ongoing government support for academic research.

KEY ISSUES IN ORGANIZING THE DELIVERY OF SERVICES TO UNIVERSITIES AND INDUSTRY

If the aim is to maximize the effectiveness of interactions between universities and industry, and within universities, *what is the best way to organize delivery of these services?* In considering this important question, institutions must also address more specific questions:

- *Should we centralize or decentralize?* Centralization brings the opportunity to create critical mass of expertise, ensure consistency and control, and effectively deploy scarce resources, whereas distributed resources result in a better understanding of local issues, improved provision of services, and local engagement.
- *Should we operate as a business or a service?* The university must determine if it is more important to make money for the institution or to provide services (and to whom). If making money is not the objective, then an alternative metric of success must be determined.

- Should any or all of the services be provided by an arm's-length, separately incorporated entity, or should they be offered through an internal university department?
- What is the best mechanism to provide these services across multiple institutions such as multiple campuses, or between a university and an affiliated teaching hospital?
- How do you balance the academic need to create new knowledge through the conduct of world-class research with the region's demand for local relevance—particularly if local problems may be mundane and not of academic interest?
- Which organizational structure provides the optimal use of resources, enables the highest level of productivity and customer service, and results in the greatest impact?

Companies expect academic institutions to operate like corporations: professional and businesslike in their dealings, flexible and eager to exploit opportunities, and responsive to the needs of their customers. It makes sense to them to create strong relationships and then exploit these relationships in as many ways as possible (for example, across multiple modalities, for the mutual benefit of both parties). The integration of services into a one-stop shop simplifies the process for company management, researchers and staff, and it promotes access to students, research facilities, expertise, and technology. For the university, one-stop shopping to faculty allows effective leveraging of the relationship across education, research support, technology transfer, and philanthropy. It also allows both parties to go beyond a single transactional experience with each other and to build longer-lasting and more meaningful relationships.

THE UNIVERSITY OF BRITISH COLUMBIA'S UNIVERSITY-INDUSTRY LIAISON OFFICE: A CASE STUDY

British Columbia has a population of 4.2 million, with 80 percent located in a concentrated area around Vancouver—a city acknowledged as one of the nicest places to live on the planet and which consistently places first or second in Mercer's quality of life index. It is a resource-based economy built on forestry, mining, fishing, and tourism—industries with minimal history in investing in research. During the past fifteen years, a high-technology sector has emerged in British Columbia with subsectors in the areas of information and communication(s) technology, biotechnology, new media, and alternative energy. Total sector performance, however, only accounts for 3.6 percent of provincial gross domestic product. Vancouver was formerly home to the Vancouver Stock Exchange which later merged into the TSX Venture Exchange. These activities helped foster a culture of risk in capital investment in the province.

The University of British Columbia (UBC) is one of Canada's premier public research institutions. With twenty-five thousand undergraduate students, sixty-five hundred graduate students, and twenty-one hundred faculty members, it is British Columbia's largest university and offers a comprehensive program of undergraduate, graduate, and professional degrees.

UBC's University-Industry Liaison Office (UILO) is an example of a one-stop shop, providing an integrated suite of services including managing all industry-sponsored research and government contract negotiations, technology transfer, and entrepreneurship. It serves university faculty and students at UBC's primary campus in Vancouver, as well as at its new campus in the Okanagan (three hundred miles east of Vancouver) and the university's five affiliated teaching hospitals.

The office was created over twenty years ago and is now recognized as the top technology transfer office in Canada and a leader in North America. A 2006 report from the Milken Institute placed UBC eighth in North America for commercialization; a 2005 report in *The Scientist* ranked UBC ninth in North America in terms of "patent power." UBC is also publicly acclaimed as the birthplace of the B.C. biotechnology industry—a sector that currently ranks seventh in North America in terms of the number and market capitalization of companies.

UILO has grown from an office of three staff primarily focused on patenting and licensing in 1984, to a fully integrated office of forty professionals organized into three main divisions: Sponsored Research Group, Technology Transfer Group, and Management and Administration Group. In addition, new opportunities are facilitated through a series of initiatives that include International Business Development, New Venture Program, Flintbox™ (an online system that enables access and dissemination of research results), and an active education program.

The Sponsored Research Group (SRG) consists of eleven staff responsible for all of the sponsored research agreements between the university and industry including grants, collaborative research agreements, service contracts, research chairs, and network and affiliation agreements. They also negotiate all government contracts. SRG manages approximately twelve hundred industry agreements per year worth about $50 million. The following are specific characteristics of the group.

- It negotiates agreements on behalf of both the university and the affiliated teaching hospitals. Each agreement lists both institutions and parties. A common set of policies governs the research agreement.
- It is organized to allow for both sectoral expertise and streaming by agreement complexity. Simple agreements have turnaround times of a few days or weeks.
- The physical proximity of the SRG staff to the technology transfer staff allows for frequent consultation and collaboration in both directions. The technology transfer staff have a better understanding of both the scientific and business aspects of the research projects, and this in turn helps the SRG staff to better identify issues of substance during negotiations. Similarly, licensing deals that include research components are also facilitated by this close proximity.

In 2006, a task force was established by UILO to examine its policies and practices related to industry-sponsored research with a focus on companies in the IT sector and issues related to intellectual property. The task force's recommendations, now fully enacted by the office, permit a more flexible approach to managing intellectual property—including the option to assign ownership to the sponsor—and put substantive control over these decisions in the hands of the faculty member. It was observed that the value of the relationships with these companies, through a multitude of mechanisms from student employment to philanthropy, far exceeded potential royalty revenues.

The Technology Transfer Group (TTG) consists of eighteen professionals that manage the technology evaluation, patenting, development, marketing, and licensing process. In a typical year they will see 160 new inventions, file two hundred patents, negotiate forty license or assignment agreements, and help spin off two to five companies. The TTG is organized by sector: life sciences, physical sciences, and information technology. Incoming technologies are assigned to the technology transfer officers that are responsible for initial assessment, preliminary marketing, and patent filing. Technologies that advance through this review are then assigned to technology managers for active development and licensing. Staff join the TTG at an entry level position of technology transfer officer, and progress through to technology transfer manager, and finally to associate director or special initiative champion. Staff recruitment, retention, and effectiveness are enhanced by a clear path for career progression, an open collegial environment, and sufficient autonomy for staff to set their own priorities and deal terms. Alumni of the TTG have gone on to run other technology transfer offices, and have accepted senior business development, corporate finance, and CEO positions for corporations.

UILO operation is spread across three locations with the main office of UILO located at UBC's Vancouver campus and satellite offices at UBC Okanagan and the affiliated teaching hospitals. These offices house both SRG and TTG staff responsible for the primary client contact with both faculty and industry. In addition, the UILO main office also provides back-office support for all locations. This includes the general support of senior management as well as staff supporting finance, administration, IT services, communications, education, and human resources. In addition, technology transfer support is provided through dedicated patent management, compliance, and legal services. The organization of UILO into a single back-office supporting multiple front offices has been particularly successful in optimizing the balance of centralization for efficiencies versus decentralization for better service.

Organizational change is fostered in three ways. First, on an annual basis both the SRG and TTG undergo an internal review and planning process which identifies issues that impede performance in emerging and growth areas for increased service. These are addressed during the subsequent year through a combination of structural change within the group, staffing and professional development, and process or procedure changes. Second, more significant challenges are addressed through the creation of a task force which has a defined mandate, term, and broad membership from the community. Third, opportunities are addressed through the creation of initiatives (International Business Development, New Venture Program, Centre for Drug Development and Delivery). These initiatives typically require distinct planning, direction, staffing and resources, and are established for a predefined period—typically two to three years. By assigning dedicated resources to these initiatives, the task force does not impede core operations. The effectiveness of each initiative is assessed annually with a formal final review. Post-initiative options include extending the term, winding down the activity, or modifying and growing the activity. As an example, the New Venture Program has come to the end of its initial tenure and is now being expanded to go beyond the UILO to a pan-university program. By institutionalizing the process for change management, it promotes the UILO as a dynamic organization that is responsive to the changing needs of its clients and adaptive to its changing environment.

KEY SUGGESTIONS FOR ADMINISTRATORS

The following suggestions were distilled from over twenty years of experience operating a one-stop shop:

- *Establish a coordinated policy framework.* Intellectual property, industry-sponsored research, conflict of interest, management of equity, and signing authority are a few of the policies that are required to provide governance to a coordinated operation. Though these policies need to be mutually supportive, consistent, and common among multiple locations or affiliated institutions (such as teaching hospitals), care should be taken to ensure that they are not proscriptive and do allow for a limited exercise of judgment at the local level. This will encourage flexibility.

- *Make clear the primary mandate of the organization.* Is it to make money or is it to provide a service to the faculty and enable industry interaction? The service model provides greater returns over time, but requires appropriate investment up front. Service organizations can operate in a businesslike manner.
- *Select the appropriate metrics to measure the unit performance in accordance with its mandate.* If service is identified as a key part of the mandate, publish service standards and measure customer satisfaction.
- *Payoff is often seen first through an increase in sponsored research funding (industry and government), prestige, and local political support for the institution.* The lead time to self-sustainability from royalty and equity liquidation is typically greater than ten years.
- *Although organizational structures will vary (such as central versus decentralized, combined versus separate services), opportunities to provide coordinated services should be explored.* Most activities require a local presence but can be effectively supported by a common back office. For larger or distributed campuses, structure operations between a front office and back office. The front office(s) provide the primary customer contact and should have a minimum of three people to provide for local internal support and mentoring. The back office provides an infrastructure of support that includes management, operations, communications, and so on.
- *Avoid concentrating the provision of all services to a single entity—such as a single faculty or school—through a single individual.* The skill sets required to deliver services by modality are unique and occasionally mutually exclusive. Deal makers are often not good administrators. In addition, duties should be organized in a manner that allows for quick turnaround on straightforward matters, whereas complex negotiations may unfold over a period of months. If a single individual is responsible for both, it is easy for the turnaround time on simple matters to grow.
- *Assemble a critical mass of talent that provides a diversity of experience and allows for synergy and teaming across talent pools.* This promotes the opportunity for staff career progression as well as for lateral movement that promotes staff satisfaction, retention, and

increased knowledge and competency. Compensation must be
competitive for both recruitment and retention.
- *Trust in your staff*. Empower them to make good decisions
  rather than strictly enforcing policies and approval processes.
  Provide them with supportive senior administration and afford
  them with the freedom to be flexible (and accountable)
  through the application of good judgment facilitated by a
  toolkit of options.
- *Encourage organizational entrepreneurship.* At the organizational
  level, this can be achieved through the use of time-bound
  initiatives to explore alternative approaches or emerging areas.
  At the individual level, empower the individual through a
  toolkit of options, flexibility, judgment, freedom to operate,
  and tolerating mistakes. Make constant change and adaptation
  part of the office culture and practice.
- *Assess operations and initiatives on a regular basis.* Learn from the
  assessments and adjust operations accordingly.

Conclusion

The success of a one-stop shop is based on a coordinated approach
to addressing the often divergent needs of industry and university
researchers. Developing these relationships remains an ongoing
process that, although reliant on a coordinated set of policies,
also requires continual review and change in order to remain
responsive to the evolving needs of industry and the research
community. The creation of an environment that encourages
talented staff to work together across modalities is vital for the
one-stop shop approach to not only be helpful to industry, but
also to provide assistance to faculty. In doing so this approach
has proved to be an effective way for the university to strengthen
university-industry relations.

CHAPTER SEVEN

UNIVERSITY-RELATED START-UP COMPANIES

Kenneth D. Walters

University-based start-up companies are a powerful and visible example of the value of university research and of the creativity and innovative talent found in universities. This chapter outlines specific steps that universities can take to develop and nurture an entrepreneurial culture among faculty and students and to increase the number of start-ups.

AUTM reports that some 4,543 companies were spun off of U.S. universities between 1980 and 2004, including biotechnology giants Amgen and Genentech, computer science–based Lycos and PayPal, and internet pioneers Google and Yahoo. These and thousands of other firms have generated great wealth and tens of thousands of high-paying jobs, transforming economic sectors in cities and regions across North America.

University-related start-ups have indeed become part of a Holy Grail of state and regional economic development strategies. In 2000, Federal Reserve Chairman Alan Greenspan told the National Governors' Association that America's universities had become an economic locomotive: "Our universities are envied around the world . . . . The payoffs—in terms of the flow of expertise, newbreak products, and start-up companies, for example—have been impressive." Greenspan's remarks were widely reported, and it is no surprise politicians and governments throughout the world look at U.S. research universities as engines of entrepreneurship and economic diversification. Every nation aspires to replicate Silicon Valley, as do regions and states in the United States that yearn to build or boost high-tech sectors and create high-paying jobs.

Despite the impressive successes of Stanford and M.I.T. in generating start-ups, regions do not require a Stanford or M.I.T. to spawn important companies. Many public research universities have a solid record of producing start-ups, as the AUTM data show.

Certainly the past thirty years of start-ups from the University of Washington (UW) have confirmed that public research universities can be entrepreneurial. To track the impact of UW research on start-ups, I was commissioned to perform an annual survey of UW-related start-up companies in the mid-1990s by the UW Office of Research. In 2000, I inventoried UW-related start-ups and the Office of Research published the report, *University of Washington: Engine of the Knowledge-Based Economy*. The report demonstrated that UW-related start-up companies grew during the 1980s and especially the 1990s—creating thousands of jobs, over $2 billion in sales revenues, hundreds of innovative products and services, and significant shareholder value. The companies stimulated economic development in numerous technology-based sectors and played a significant role in diversifying the state's economy.

A further study in 2003, *Creating the Future: University of Washington-Related Startup Companies, 1973–2003*, updated UW's strong track record for start-ups. Most surprising was the finding that growth in start-ups continued even after the high-flying 1990s, only slightly diminished through the economic slowdown of 2001–2003. *Creating the Future* documented that research expenditures by start-ups were a kind of "economic stabilizer" to a region's economy, preserving innovation during downturns in venture capital and new private investment. Even in the post-bubble environment UW-related companies were launched at the rate of a dozen companies per year, and research expenditures of existing university-related start-ups continued to add significantly to the region's R&D reputation and employment.

As of 2007, well over two hundred companies have come out of UW research and intellectual property. The purpose of this chapter is to spell out what we can learn from this thirty-year period of success at the University of Washington.

Why Are Start-Ups Important?

Why do university faculty and students start companies when it may be easier to license technologies to existing firms? There are business reasons, personal reasons, and public interest reasons. First, early-stage technologies are not always transferable to large firms, due to high risks or expected long development time lines. Second, some faculty and student researchers have entrepreneurial genes or zeal, or both, and want to control the development of their technologies and creative ideas. Third, academic spin-offs generate wealth, create jobs, keep talent in the region, produce innovative new products and services, attract new investment and research, diversify the economy, and generally benefit the public in numerous economic and social ways.

Aside from these reasons, several powerful *academic* arguments exist for university-spawned start-ups:

1. Universities want to encourage entrepreneurship by faculty, staff, and students and are justifiably proud of their entrepreneurial accomplishments.
2. The companies provide research dollars to the university; for example, one UW spin-off brought a $9 million research agreement to UW.
3. Presidents and administrators look for opportunities to tell legislators, businesspeople, and the public about the relevance of the university research and academic programs; start-ups are an excellent vehicle for this message.
4. Start-up executives and entrepreneurs sit on advisory boards for university programs and typically are powerful advocates of the university's programs. A luminary such as biotech legend George Rathmann, founding CEO of both Amgen and Icos, is an advocate of research programs in the community and with legislators.
5. Faculty returning from successful start-ups after leaves of absence are often more inspired and energized as teachers. One UW department chair reported that one of his faculty entrepreneurs was "transformed" as a teacher after he came back from a successful start-up.

6. CEOs of university start-ups help as advisors and networking agents on future technology transfer deals.
7. University programs devoted to start-ups, such as multitenant facilities and business incubators and accelerators, constitute an entrepreneurship teaching lab for students.
8. Taking small equity stakes in start-ups can become valuable at a later stage, as shown in numerous cases.

DEFINING UNIVERSITY-RELATED START-UPS

University-related start-up companies are community enterprises, not strictly "university" companies. Many different relationships can exist between these companies and the university. An accurate list of close university relationships with start-ups should include:

- Companies founded on technology licensed from a university
- Companies founded by university faculty, staff, or students around their university-based research
- Companies reconstituted around university technology (a very small percentage of university-related start-ups)
- Companies where university faculty play a seminal scientific role
- Companies where faculty, based on their research expertise, drive initial product development

Note that this list includes some start-ups that are not formal "outputs" of the university's technology transfer office. At UW, technology licensing staff members assist faculty and graduate students in birthing companies, even when no university license or intellectual property is involved. The technology transfer professionals steer faculty and students to capable and trustworthy businesspeople and entrepreneurs, and even help faculty identify and strategize on business planning, financing options, and legal resources.

The broad definition of university-related start-ups given above also demonstrates that the impact of university research on entrepreneurship is far greater than the formal start-up statistics reported to AUTM, which stress companies formed by licenses to start-ups. We also underestimate spin-off activity from universities when we overlook "back door" companies. What has been called "guerrilla tech transfer" is, from the author's discussions with tech transfer professionals, a significant economic activity and is a further indication of the economic and societal value of university research.

Drivers for Start-Ups

Six major factors account for the dramatic increase in university-based start-up activity over the past thirty years:

1. Increases in university leadership, support, and encouragement of start-up ventures that arise from the university's research—support which is palpable at UW.

2. Biotechnology research, stemming from commercial applications of revolutionary work on recombinant DNA thirty years ago, a process still in its early stages of development.

3. The expansion of intellectual property rights in the 1980 U.S. Supreme Court case, *Diamond v. Chakrabarty*, which granted patent status to biological life forms.

4. The 1980 Bayh-Dole Act granting universities ownership of the fruits of federally funded faculty research, and stipulating that university licensing to start-up companies is national policy.

5. The explosion of new financial mechanisms for entrepreneurial ventures, including venture capital, SBIR/STTR (Small Business Innovation Research grants and Small Business Technology Transfer Research grants) programs, foundation support for research, research parks, business incubators and accelerators, and other new institutional developments to stimulate commercialization.

6. Beefed-up university entrepreneurship programs—not just isolated courses for business students but programs extending across the campus to engineering, computer science, medicine, dentistry, nursing, the physical sciences, liberal arts, social sciences, and throughout the professional schools. The Kauffman Foundation continues to stimulate this trend through its encouragement of across-the-campus entrepreneurship education.

UNIVERSITIES AND HIGH-TECH ENTREPRENEURSHIP

America is the land of opportunity where new Horatio Alger stories happen daily. People of modest backgrounds blaze paths to sometimes spectacular success and wealth. But some U.S. regions are more entrepreneurial than others, especially in technology. Discussions of high-tech success start with the San Francisco Bay area, but many other areas including Seattle, San Diego, Boston, and Austin continue to provide insights into growing high-tech entrepreneurial success.

The Seattle experience and the role of UW in nurturing over two hundred start-ups spawned from UW research is an especially useful case study. In thirty years UW has helped to transform Seattle and the Puget Sound region from an economy based on fishing, aerospace, and forest products into a high-tech center of some sophistication and scientific diversity. A significant part of UW's role was in developing and integrating four ingredients required for high-tech entrepreneurial success.

1. BUILD THE RESEARCH BASE

Science and technology are a kind of wealth, although unmeasured in formal national economic statistics. University faculty and students help create this wealth, which in the twenty-first century translates into an economy that is increasingly complex and technology driven. High-tech entrepreneurship starts with research. As Milken Institute studies show, the presence of major research institutions is the single most critical factor for regional high-tech economic success.

Over the past thirty years the research capabilities of UW have dramatically grown to over $1 billion in external research funding, making UW the top U.S. public university recipient of federal research dollars. The role of this research in UW entrepreneurship is apparent when one looks at twenty-five economic sectors and niche markets in the state of Washington that have been expanded and energized by UW-related start-up companies:

1. Advanced materials
2. Advertising data analysis
3. Agricultural biotechnology

4. Bioremediation
5. Cell phone microchips
6. Chemometrics
7. Computer graphics
8. Educational and training software
9. Food safety and testing
10. Fuel cells
11. Genetic testing
12. Geological and seismic software
13. Image processing and video streaming
14. Instrumentation
15. Intelligent Internet shopping agents
16. Interactive conferencing
17. Manufacturing systems
18. Medical devices
19. Medical diagnostics
20. Medical therapeutics
21. Microsensors and biosensors
22. Neurosurgery
23. Research tools
24. Security systems
25. Statistical analysis and decision-making software

Two conclusions can be drawn. First, the companies in nearly all these sectors are conceived or firmly rooted in university research. Second, scarcely any of these UW-spawned companies would have been birthed out of business schools or out of business plans developed by MBA or undergraduate business students working on their own. Most required a research-intensive environment focused on technology development such as can only be found in a research university with strong science and engineering programs and graduate professional schools. These research strengths, in turn, should be linked to technology-focused entrepreneurship programs, either located in the business school or on other parts of campus.

2. WORK WITH COMMUNITY ENTREPRENEURS

Science is necessary but not sufficient for high-tech entrepreneurship. Academic researchers, assiduously focused on their specialties, can be unschooled in new venture development. Business start-ups require someone from the inside who knows business planning, new venture mechanics, how to raise capital, and how to build a new product development team. Newly minted MBAs from a major business school rarely have this expertise. In fact, a skilled manager from a successful corporate bureaucracy may not be what the nascent firm needs. The new university-based start-up needs a CEO with entrepreneurial skills—who is often someone with experience with start-ups.

Case studies of UW start-ups show that the entrepreneurial CEO in a start-up must be skilled at seed planting, tin cupping, horse trading, sanity checking, and team building. The entrepreneur should have a synthesized vision that includes foresight (sees the market and the vision); global view (world competitive view); depth perception (sees responses from competitors); peripheral vision (understands responses from competitors); and revision (can change course as the start-up progresses). The entrepreneurial CEO must then sell the vision, find funding, be comfortable with new venture mechanics and operations, and build the initial engineering and business team. University tech transfer offices should be networked in the community and often can help faculty find entrepreneurs for their start-ups.

3. UTILIZE THE DIVERSE SOURCES OF FUNDING

Funding for a new company comes from three possible sources—customers, grantors, and investors. The UW experience shows that a major development of the past three decades is the proliferation of funding sources for start-ups:

a. *Government research grants* helped launch many UW spin-offs. In fact, numerous companies could not have survived infancy without government research grants. One firm, started by two engineering students, raised money from the National Science Foundation. Another received a $2 million grant from the Department of Commerce for development of fuel cells.

b. *SBIR and STTR grants* provide important funding for early-stage technology development to literally scores of university start-ups.

c. *State-funded programs*, such as the Washington Technology Center, provide small grants to small businesses in the state. Over thirty UW-related start-ups have received grants through this state program.

d. The Washington Research Foundation, a *seed capital fund*, has helped launched many UW-related start-ups.

e. *Venture capital* firms invest in UW-related technologies, although the post-2000 financial environment has been somewhat less auspicious than the earlier decade.

f. The availability of *angel capital* and the Alliance of Angels, the Seattle-based angel capital network, has helped launch many UW-related companies. Wealthy individuals who take an interest in emerging technology start-ups are truly "angels" to these ventures and to economic diversification.

g. Faculty and student entrepreneurs tap *personal savings* and persuade family and friends to invest in their new ventures. A large number of start-ups begin with this funding source.

h. *Initial public offerings* have been important to some UW-related ventures, particularly in the biotechnology and medical device fields.

i. Aside from IPOs, UW-related companies have raised funding by *follow-on stock offerings* (or other securities, typically convertible bonds) in the public capital markets.

j. A number of UW-related firms receive *foundation grants*.

k. *Large company-sponsored research* in small companies is an important funding source for many start-ups.

4. Build a Community Ecosystem of Business Know-How

A network of business professionals helping start-ups makes up a region's entrepreneurial ecosystem. Indeed, both capital and entrepreneurs gravitate to places that welcome new enterprise and understand how to address the problems that start-ups encounter. The range of issues includes all the functional aspects of business: marketing, operations, legal, finance, accounting, and business systems development.

UW start-ups have been a critical part of building the entrepreneurial ecosystem in the Puget Sound region. As a result, the business network to support new ventures in the Seattle area is much stronger today. The key is creating programs and institutions to bring these elements together, which may explain why university start-ups flourish in established hubs such as San Francisco, San Diego, Seattle, and Boston.

AN ACTION PLAN FOR ADMINISTRATORS

We conclude this chapter with a list of suggestions or action steps for university administrators and leaders.

BUILD COMPANY CLUSTERS FROM ACADEMIC STRENGTHS

Companies often evolve around sectors of special strength in a university. UW's strength in certain key technologies has been critical for UW-related spin-offs and a number of companies have spun off from each of these sectors:

a. Ultrasound
b. Biotechnology
c. Green technologies
d. Educational software and training
e. Internet software
f. Medical devices

ADMINISTRATORS CAN PROVIDE LEADERSHIP BY PUBLICIZING, TRAINING, COMMUNICATING, LEGITIMIZING, AND CHEERLEADING

University administrators—presidents, provosts, offices of research, technology transfer offices—can show support for start-ups by holding information sessions for faculty, publicizing university successes in the community, increasing on-campus visibility about the relevance of research to the private sector, and supporting faculty start-ups.

Specific examples from UW begin with the fact that for many years the president's annual address specifically mentioned technology transfer and start-ups. Under Alvin L. Kwiram, the

Office of Research published quarterly newsletters, special reports on start-up activity, the quarterly magazine *Northwest Science and Technology*, and a series of books about UW research: *Pathbreakers, UW Showcase*, and *UW Ventures*.

The UW Office of Technology Licensing under Robert C. Miller was an integral part of all these activities, and conducted training sessions across campus to show faculty how to start up companies and work with the OTL. The OTL persuaded the Business School to start new programs on technology entrepreneurship, helped raise private funds for the business school's entrepreneurship programs, and encouraged new entrepreneurship initiatives in the School of Engineering, in computer science, and in the School of Medicine and the health sciences. Under Kwiram and Miller, technology transfer became highly visible throughout the UW and the president and provost provided support and updates so that the regents and the community were informed of progress.

TRAIN STUDENTS IN BUSINESS PLANNING AND MARKET RESEARCH

Scientists can ignore marketing and may even deplore it. They are so focused on research and technology development that they have to be forced to think about markets, costs, customers, and operational business issues, and may even regard these issues as unnecessary. The starting point in overcoming this oversight is to allow and encourage faculty start-ups to get the typically free assistance of MBA students, perhaps teamed with other graduate students, in business planning and market analysis. Early-stage companies desperately need this expertise and can benefit from business planning and market research studies from the beginning.

SET UP ENTREPRENEURSHIP CENTERS THAT FOCUS ON LAB-TO-MARKET ISSUES AND NEW VENTURE MECHANICS

Traditional entrepreneurship courses can neglect technology start-ups as this is not the zone of expertise for most business faculty and students. Technology-driven companies or firms that are likely to emerge from research labs have unique challenges ("cool" technologies, long incubation periods, heavy and drawn-out capital requirements, and uncertain markets). It is easier to help a student write a business plan for a new frozen yogurt stand than for a nascent company in proteomics or neurosurgery. Entrepreneurship programs need to be responsive to the needs not only of students but also of faculty and graduate student researchers.

Many exciting new programs are being established in business schools. Pierre Lassonde, an MBA alumnus of the University of Utah, recently gave $13.25 million to the university to establish a program to allow and encourage business students to collaborate with the university's researchers to commercialize new technologies while earning credit from the business school. The program, initiated in 1999, has been so successful that a handful of biotechnology companies have been spun off and the new endowment in 2006 will greatly expand the program.

Encourage and Utilize "Serial" Entrepreneurs

University-based entrepreneurs who earn $1 million—or $10 million or $100 million—from one or more successful start-ups rarely rest on the laurels of their achievement, even if they leave the university environment. They keep seeing new opportunities and starting new companies. Examples at UW include David Auth, Leroy Hood, Kirk Beach, Roy Martin, Dan Weld, Oren Etzioni, and Joseph Garbini. The lesson for universities is that serial entrepreneurs can be the gift that keeps on giving. They are a resource to be used for new ventures and new research programs.

Encourage Student Entrepreneurship—Student Companies Are Infectious and Eminently Newsworthy

Over forty companies have been started by UW students based on their research work at the university. Student entrepreneurs have the frequent effect of influencing each other and stimulating ideas for more companies from their peers. In particular, the rise of cross-campus entrepreneurship programs has meant that students in one department (say, electrical engineering) can evoke new ideas from students in other departments (such as biomedical engineering). Medical students at UW are found competing in new venture ideas, and entrepreneurship has sprouted up in schools and departments as dispersed as the Jackson School of International Studies, child development and mental retardation, chemistry, nursing, oceanography, geophysics, forestry, and speech and hearing sciences.

LOOK EVERYWHERE: IDIOSYNCRATIC IDEAS AND TECHNOLOGIES CAN CREATE COMPANIES

This guideline may seem to contradict the advice to build areas of research strength and encourage "star" faculty who are serial entrepreneurs, but it is complementary, not inconsistent. Idiosyncratic research can lead to exotic technologies and successful companies. UW scientists study the biology of Puget Sound, and several companies have been formed based on this expertise. One uses the discarded shells of crustaceans (crab and oysters) to produce a variety of products such as swimming pool cleaners, nutraceuticals, and other exotic products. Another, a marine biotechnology company, uses seaweed to produce patented marine algae extracts to make skin and hair conditioners. Every university has faculty doing important work, and technology transfer offices should be creative in helping these faculty find entrepreneurial outlets for their research.

HIRE TECHNOLOGY TRANSFER STAFF WHO CAN HELP FACULTY

Technology licensing officers are critical to a university's success with start-ups. The faculty initially report invention disclosures to them, and they need to give wise counsel about business options, provide accurate information about university policies, and must generally encourage entrepreneurial faculty to pursue their visions while operating within university guidelines.

When Lee Huntsman, former president of UW, was associate dean of medicine, he appointed John Des Rosier to be director of industry liaison. Des Rosier excelled at several tasks: (1) setting up university-industry relations, (2) facilitating start-ups by faculty,

(3) educating faculty about entrepreneurial activities and university policies, and (4) encouraging faculty to be entrepreneurial.

Similarly, Gerald Barnett, who built the software and copyright ventures group at the Office of Intellectual Property and Technology Transfer at UW, was a peripatetic helper to faculty across campus. Barnett is particularly gifted in seeing out-of-the-box possibilities or creative business models for a product or venture from research programs. Scores of faculty were nurtured by his advice and encouraged to find innovative ways to develop markets for their research. Partly as a result of many of Barnett's creative ideas, software and copyright ventures have grown nationally to be an increasingly important piece of the portfolios of university intellectual property.

DON'T GIVE UP EASILY; FAILURES OFTEN PRECEDE SUCCESS

Start-ups are not for the fainthearted, and numerous examples at UW show that though a faculty member's first foray into start-ups may fail, subsequent efforts succeed. Sometimes a second start-up company tries a new approach, new management, new markets, or new technologies. In short, it is common for faculty and students to move on to the next research project or hot topic, and a new start-up follows. Just as with college athletics, there are losses—which are sometimes followed by championships. In the world of high-tech entrepreneurship, failure can be a prelude to success even while success in one venture never guarantees subsequent success.

DON'T IGNORE SMALL SUCCESSES; SMALL MARKETS ARE IMPORTANT

Many university start-ups never go public and never are acquired by larger firms, but that does not mean they may not be nice little businesses. A number of UW spin-offs never have reached $10 million or $100 million in sales, but a company that continually generates $250,000 or $2 million in annual sales can be a real financial success.

Use Cash Flow to Finance New Products

University start-ups often begin with one product. There is a temptation to live a happy life with the cash flow from that product, but a number of spin-offs wisely decide early to reinvest profits in new product development—a strategy which has proven to be critical for long-run success. Companies with extremely modest beginnings have used cash flow to continually fund ambitious R&D programs and invest in new products. This has not only maintained their relationship to the university but also promoted growth in sales and employment.

When Troubles Arise, Look for New Markets

Start-ups frequently develop technical and research problems and are tempted to just quit. But others tweak their technologies and reinvent themselves, finding new markets and achieving eventual success. Technologies often have multiple uses, but those uses have to be found or invented—they are not always apparent at first. UW companies that changed markets in response to setbacks include ICOS, Micronics, and Microprobe—and many more examples could be added.

Stay Patient; Technology Development Takes Years

Biotechnology and indeed nearly all medical technologies take longer to reach the market than originally planned. Though some eventually fail, what is surprising is that after a decade or more a number of UW spin-offs have eventually succeeded, after years and years of R&D and effort.

Conclusion

University research continually breeds a flow of new and important firms—creating value, stimulating growth, promoting regional diversification, and keeping talent in a region. The exciting news is that universities are evolving new "systems" for nurturing entrepreneurship. More universities are increasing their support for campus start-ups. Local investors and entrepreneurs are working more closely with technology licensing offices. Business schools are newly energized to see business opportunities from research and new technology. We are still at an early stage in developing these new systems. Although universities should never promise miracles in economic development, the UW experience shows that important strides can be made to increase entrepreneurial start-ups and dramatically benefit a region and the state.

CHAPTER EIGHT

UNIVERSITY-AFFILIATED RESEARCH PARKS

Mark Betteridge

There is a natural and challenging tension between helping start-up companies and making sufficient money as a research park—both must succeed. The research park management and board must establish and nurture trust with the higher learning institution that is helping to create start-up companies, while the institution must appreciate that the research park is accepting much of the risk inherent in providing expensive real estate to companies with little or no commercial track record. The best models emphasize a full arm's-length research park structure.

University-affiliated research parks (UARP) are developments designed to work synergistically with neighboring institutions of higher learning. The Association of University Research Parks (AURP) Web site states that these research parks are property-based ventures that have "master planned property and buildings designed primarily for private/public research and development facilities, high technology and science based companies and support services." The mission of university research parks varies according to location, and missions have evolved over time. In several instances UARPs were designed to generate revenue for the host university through land leases. In others they were heavily supported by the state as a vehicle for economic development. In yet a third set, the original objective was to create space for the development of start-up companies arising from university-based research. In most instances the mission has been altered due to changes in board membership, financial circumstances, or local politics.

The Stanford Research Park, started in 1951, is considered by many to be the first high-tech research park and was instrumental in the growth of Silicon Valley. Its first lessee was Varian Associates. Today, approximately 150 companies employ twenty-three thousand people on seven hundred acres of land in this park. Other examples of prominent research parks, among many, include Research Triangle Park in North Carolina; Alumni Research Fund Park in Madison, Wisconsin; and the Arizona Science and Technology Park in Tucson, Arizona. These parks have all won the annual Association of University Research Park Outstanding Research/Science Park Achievement Award.

The factors that determine success of UARPs are as varied as the original and current missions. For example, the success of the Stanford Research Park was stimulated by several factors including its proximity to a great research university, the availability of a large piece of land that could be used to create a critical mass of companies, and the emergence of the semiconductor industry with Fairchild Semiconductor's development of the first planar integrated circuit in 1959. Research Triangle Park, conversely, was developed under the guidance of a group of dedicated local citizens that stimulated investment by the state in the development of the park for the benefit of the regional economy. The plan was to recruit companies that would place major research operations in the park. As of 2002, the park consisted of seventy-eight hundred acres and was home to 119 R&D-related organizations. In addition, there now are a wide range of service organizations located there. Of the 38,500 people working there in 2002, 82 percent were employed by multinational corporations, and they occupied over 19 million square feet of developed space.

The Association of University Research Parks (AURP) provides an outstanding Web site that defines other useful characteristics of these parks and provides extensive survey data regarding the missions and nature of a variety of research parks in North America. For the purposes of this book, this chapter will emphasize one of the characteristics that is most valuable to the technology transfer capabilities of universities: the ability to provide space for start-up companies derived from university-based research. As mentioned in a previous chapter, start-ups are an excellent mode of technology transfer, provide revenue to the university in the form of research funds and equity, and can serve as a first-rate training environment for students. The example we use here is Discovery Parks, Inc. (DPI), in Vancouver, British Columbia, Canada. DPI was also a winner of the AURP Outstanding Research/Science Achievement Award and is an excellent example of a private company managing commercial real estate assets in the interests of a university and the local community. The majority of research parks that won this prestigious award are managed by similar structures.

DPI has been a major factor in the development of technology-intensive companies in the greater Vancouver area since 1992. DPI became a significant element in successful technology transfer programs of the regional universities through the development of space for emerging technology-intensive companies. A list of the achievements of DPI is summarized at the close of this chapter. The author has been a senior executive at the helm of DPI since it originated.

History

Discovery Parks was created by the government of British Columbia in 1979. Although initially a foundation, Discovery had a real estate company, a venture capital firm, and the capacity to market and promote itself. The original constitution from 1979 is still valid, even prescient. In summary form, it stated:

Discovery is created:

a. To operate, without profit to its members, for the benefit of the people of British Columbia, and in particular for the benefit of universities, Provincial institutes and the Science Council, by receiving funds and other assets from senior governments and any other sources;

b. To attract, foster, stimulate and participate in the development of scientific and technological industries, skills and expertise, and related management skills, which will create employment opportunities for graduates of universities and Provincial institutes, through the encouragement and assistance of industrial research and scientific and technological research and development;

c. To provide suitable buildings, and generally to help create a favorable climate for scientific and technological research and development for the purpose of stimulating the establishment and growth of scientific and technological industries, skills and expertise having local and world markets.

d. To work towards broadening and strengthening the economic base of the Province of British Columbia.

PHASE I: DISCOVERY PARKS 1979 TO 1990—A QUASI-GOVERNMENT ORGANIZATION

The named beneficiaries of Discovery were the University of British Columbia, Simon Fraser University, the University of Victoria, the British Columbia Institute of Technology, and the Science Council of British Columbia. Discovery was structured such that each of these institutions had the right to nominate someone to the board(s). In practice, this meant that the president of the institution sat on the foundation board and the vice president of research sat on the operating company board (Discovery Parks Incorporated). In addition, the boards had many other members, from various sectors, appointed by the provincial government bringing the total board membership to over twenty members at times.

The Original Endowment

The government of British Columbia endowed Discovery with eighty acres of serviced land in Burnaby, a suburb of Vancouver, and funded the construction of an initial incubator of about one hundred thousand square feet. In addition, assistance was given to Discovery to negotiate leases of land (approximately seventy acres each) on the campuses of the University of British Columbia (UBC) and Simon Fraser University (SFU). These land leases included performance targets for building appropriate buildings by given dates in the 1980s. Although a telecomm R&D facility was built on the SFU Discovery Parks site and a pulp and paper research facility (PAPRICAN) at UBC, the development targets were not met, technically putting Discovery into default. In hindsight, the original target of an incubator on each campus was extremely optimistic, given that the Discovery Foundation operating budget was based on the initial lease revenues that were used to support both real estate and venture capital operating expenses.

The Venture Capital Fund

During the initial phase of the Discovery Foundation, the board and management team placed heavy emphasis on Discovery Enterprises, the venture capital arm of the foundation. In British Columbia, this was in the early days of the VC industry and applied to the whole notion of commercializing intellectual property emanating from postsecondary institutions. Several technology companies were founded and grown during this period, within the Discovery system as well as separate from it, but the VC investments made by Discovery were, overall, in the negative. Because the financial resources of the Foundation were committed to this activity, the beneficiaries (the four institutions) were seeing little or no financial or other benefit to their technology transfer programs.

In order to meet the technology transfer objectives of Discovery and the universities, the Foundation was restructured to emphasize construction of space appropriate for the development of university spin-off companies and other research-intensive companies wishing to locate their research operations near the universities. The beneficiary institutions worked with the provincial government to remove reporting requirements between Discovery and the province. The venture capital function of Discovery was closed, leaving a smaller board focused primarily on managing the real estate assets. With the understanding that no further funding would be received from the province, Discovery became a private organization. By law, assets remained the property of the foundation (a charity) but management was carried out by Discovery Parks Incorporated, and the two-board system referred to above remained. The operational goal became the construction of at least one building on each beneficiary institution's campus, which would reflect the tech transfer policies and the demand at each site. Each building was planned and financed privately, with the goal of generating operating profits after a reasonable level of occupancy.

Risk Transfer

From this time forward, Discovery acted to transfer legal, financial, or political risk away from the four institutions and the senior governments. In particular, Discovery Parks was responsible for collecting rents and enforcing leases. This is a process that frequently causes concern for universities when someone's favorite company is in default. In addition Discovery was responsible for raising capital and managing debt. Discovery had become a private organization that was required to use its own balance sheet and business acumen to build equity, raise commercial debt, and operate profitably. This ensured that any debt for campus buildings at one university could not affect Discovery debt on the campus of another university (that is, no cross-collateralization). Consequently, Discovery managed affairs for each university without potential detriment to the affairs of another. Even though the universities were not responsible for any debt, the primary detriment envisaged was ineffective operation of space for local spin-off companies, as spin-off companies were seen as important tech transfer.

Phase II: 1990 to 2000 — Raising Equity and Development on All Campuses

The new boards have roughly equal representation from the beneficiary institutions and the private sector. Although the Constitution remained in place, the board of Discovery Parks Incorporated decided that its prime objective was to create suitable buildings on each of the four campuses to meet the emerging needs of the host institutions' technology transfer programs. Each site had different aims, strengths, and goals.

Contract Management

At the same time, the board decided to hire a contract manager of the assets rather than having employees. It hired what was then the relatively new University of British Columbia Real Estate Corporation in order to gain access to its management team. UBC Real Estate had been created by the University of British Columbia as a private, for-profit, stand-alone company in 1987 to generate equity from the development of campus lands. The first major project comprised twenty-six acres of campus land that was committed to almost one thousand multifamily housing units (townhouses and apartments). The land was serviced and subdivided into eleven parcels with each being "sold" on a ninety-nine-year land lease to private housing developers. Individual housing units on these long-term lease lands were sold to the general public at market prices by the private developers at no risk to the institution. Total net profits to UBC from this project exceeded $80 million.

Rezoning Discovery's Original Land Endowment in the Suburbs

Using this management team, the business plan for Discovery Parks became the rezoning of the original land endowment in Burnaby to extract capital that could be used as the equity for financing tech transfer–capable buildings on the various campuses. As equity was generated and combined with commercial mortgage borrowing, facilities were to be built on each campus and increased according to need.

The first challenge was to rezone the Burnaby lands, assets that could be converted to capital for construction on the campuses. This required changing the perception of the local municipality as the original zoning envisioned a government employee environment rather than private enterprises. It took almost three years to effect this transition, but once done, and in a rising real estate market for this type of property, Discovery developed and sold numerous buildings for a full range of sizes and types of technology-related firms. Most of these projects were then sold for capital gains to provide the equity for the on-campus buildings that would house start-up companies based on faculty research.

It is worth emphasizing again that the debt for this work was an obligation of Discovery Parks and not an obligation of the beneficiary institutions or any form of government. Effectively, Discovery has acted as a risk transfer mechanism with the benefits flowing to the beneficiary institutions.

Unique Lab Building Design

Discovery created a cost-effective and flexible generic design for the on-campus buildings. It is wet-lab capable but can be used for almost any form of office or lab. This design was adapted for all campus buildings developed under this strategy and it has proven effective. This design has subsequently been used in other locations in North America. One big advantage of the design is that the space is cost effective for start-ups and can be reconfigured when tenants change or as companies grow out of the available space and move out. Moreover, the space can be reconfigured from biotech to info tech and back again.

The Market Peak

By the end of the 1990s, and just prior to the "dot-com crash," Discovery had negotiated land leases on each of the campuses and built at least one building on each to meet the needs of the host institution's approach to tech transfer. A large proportion of the original endowment in Burnaby was converted into equity and several large tech-related companies occupied the buildings on these lands. Discovery built two facilities for multitenant uses on these lands in order to assist smaller companies that did not benefit from being on a campus. One of these buildings used a pioneering ground-source heat pump system that has become a model for an energy efficient or green environment.

In several instances, tenant companies outgrew the on-campus facilities, especially at UBC. Consequently, Discovery either developed a facility for them on the Burnaby lands or, in one case, purchased a site in Vancouver for what became a very successful biotech firm. Strategically, these relatively high-risk business decisions helped to keep these firms in the local economy and is an additional form of economic development contemplated in the original constitution. These activities reinforce the value of the legal structure of Discovery with the absence of risk for the universities.

By 2000, Discovery had developed more than a million square feet of buildings on and off campuses. It had acquired from a local telecomm firm another one hundred thousand square feet located in one of the on-campus sites and had renovated and operated an old federal research lab on a campus. At any time, there were about sixty tenants and owners of space in the six locations. Supply of suitable and affordable space more than met the needs on the campuses. Discovery had become adept in providing cost-effective space for early-stage firms on each campus site. Net profits generated at each campus, treating each as a separate profit center, were donated to the vice president of research of each university. Almost all business risk was covered by Discovery with essentially no recourse to the institution or the provincial government.

Phase III: 2000 to 2005—Consolidation

In this period, Discovery transferred almost all of its assets into a trust as a precautionary measure for tax purposes. At the same time, membership on the board of this trust was moved under the control of the trustees, thereby increasing its independence. The trust and the assets are no longer the property of the foundation nor controlled by it.

By 2003, Discovery had built more than enough facilities on and off campuses to satisfy the market. This included Canada's first LEED-certified lab building, one that meets an international green sustainable standard that is gaining prominence.

Shift to Strategic Planning for the Future of Technology

From 2000 to the present, the prime business objectives have been to increase occupancy; refinance debt at lower rates as opportunities arise; and to work closely with industry associations, the postsecondary institutions, angel and VC investors, local politicians, and others with a stake in the future of the technology industries. Discovery personnel have become more active with all of these groups and with local economic development agencies as the linkages among all of these actors became more important. This activity helped keep technology a prominent part of the economic development policies of all levels of government at a time when real estate, mining, and other commodity-based industries became dominant forces in the cyclical economy of British Columbia.

By 2005, Discovery started to examine seriously whether provision of specialized real estate assets should be the prime function of the trust. At the same time, the commercial and industrial real estate markets in this region have seen significant decreases in vacancy and considerable increases in rental rates with almost nobody else providing the type of space for which Discovery has become known.

By fall of 2006, Discovery had sold almost all of its freehold assets to raise capital in a very strong market and to reduce debt. On campus, Discovery sold one of its buildings to the host institution that wanted it for other purposes. As the residential real estate markets across North America go through cyclical and predicted downturns, the present question is whether the creation of new technology companies, on and off campus, will increase in number and size again. If so, Discovery may well resume its history of building appropriately sustainable buildings that work at market rates.

Summary of DPI Accomplishments

Between 1992 and 2006, DPI was responsible for the following accomplishments:

- Developing, operating, and owning seven tech transfer buildings on one polytechnic campus, and three university campuses on Discovery's own freehold land.
- Pioneering the design, financing, construction, and leasing of highly cost-effective, flexible wet-biotech labs for spin-off companies on campuses. This architectural model now has been adopted by other research parks.
- Providing financial support to the respective Vice Presidents of Research from the net operating profits of the real estate. Cash transfers now have exceeded $10M.
- Raising all equity and debt privately, without support from government and with virtually no risk to the host universities.
- Transferring virtually all risk, legal, financial and political, away from the host institutions while assisting in their tech transfer operations.
- Creating more than 1.5 million square feet of space for technology-intensive companies, including more than fifty university-based start-ups, thereby helping economic development in the province.

LESSONS LEARNED

First and foremost, the board and management of an enterprise such as Discovery Parks must learn to deal with ambiguity of mission. This reduces to a conflict between profit-making versus helping start-up firms. To some degree, it involves a cultural divide between commerce and academia that stems from the difference in commercial versus institutional construction standards and the generation of operating capital from building cost-effective labs. Although commercialization of intellectual property is far more accepted and practiced today than twenty years ago, most constituents of the academic world have inadequate understanding of business, particularly of economic constraints on projects developed without government funding. False expectations of free or low-cost R&D space arise in the conflicting context of large financial returns to the host universities. Therefore, an ongoing education and negotiation process with host institutions is central to the management of Discovery Parks.

Second, trust, at a personal level, is crucial. The management teams are responsible for technology development and transfer in the universities, and the management teams providing the physical facilities must continually balance the needs of the financial world with those of the academic world. In particular, the parties must work within the constraints of economic and construction realities on the one hand and the desire for space and quick financial return on the other. The two parties must work every day to build up a trusting relationship with a long-term view for success.

Third, a private enterprise with a public purpose seems to be the best management structure. Discovery Parks attempts to maintain this balance. The private aspect insures market discipline and efficiency, keeps debt and political and financial risk away from governments and institutions, and ensures the relatively fast decision making that is needed in the private finance world. The public purpose of such an enterprise can be defined by senior government representatives and officials who can then step aside while society reaps the benefits.

Concluding Remarks

Why is the Discovery Parks business model effective? The host institution gains specialized laboratory and office space to grow affiliated and spin-off companies in a building located anywhere it chooses on its campus. This building costs the host nothing other than the opportunity costs of the land that is leased to Discovery Parks. In return, the institution transfers all of the construction, financing, and operating risks to Discovery Parks and receives a fair share of the net operating profits that Discovery generates. Discovery accepts a below-market return on its investment because it exists to benefit the host institutions, not private investors. All of Discovery's profits are either reinvested in British Columbia either by way of distribution of some of the net profit to the host institution or as equity in additional similar buildings. It is a positive closed loop.

Chapter Nine

Connecting Science and Business

Mary Lindenstein Walshok

The UCSD CONNECT program was created by community leaders in partnership with the University of California, San Diego (UCSD) campus in 1985. It has been a critical contributor to the transformation of a regional economy, previously dominated by defense contracting and tourism, to a globally recognized center of high-tech and life science clusters anchored by the research institutions on the "Torrey Pines Mesa." This chapter underscores how important it is to ensure an "ecosystem of innovation" for technology commercialization and cluster development; we also look at the vital role CONNECT played in creating such an ecosystem in San Diego.

Less than forty years ago the San Diego metropolitan region was regarded by most as a sleepy second-tier city blessed with a fabulous coastal ecology, a temperate climate, and an economy fed by military contracting and tourism. Although a new campus of the University of California was being established, Dr. Jonas Salk was building his bioscience research institute in La Jolla, and John Jay Hopkins, the CEO of Convair, had just established General Atomics as a major nuclear science "think tank," no one considered the region a "tech center." San Diego had no Fortune 500 companies, no local venture capital, and only a handful of IP and corporate attorneys. It did have a hundred-year history of economic development tied to responding to the needs of the military. When science helped conclude the Second World War with the atom bomb, San Diegans zoned hundreds of acres of undeveloped land on Torrey Pines Mesa for "research and light industry" as a way to respond to the new needs of the military.

The picture today is dramatically different. The new university and the many start-up research institutes established in the 1960s and 1970s number more than two dozen and represent close to $1.8 billion annually in basic research activity. San Diego's economy has been transformed by globally competitive new economy clusters in IT, life science, and software, which supplemented the traditional defense contracting. Its business infrastructure includes significant angel networks, venture capital, global law firms with large IP practices, and a highly educated and diverse engineering, biomedical, and R&D workforce. San Diego has a growing international reputation as a leading "innovation hub" and is a major player in the international science community.

Why did a community that began in the 1960s with fewer intellectual, innovation, and technology assets than such cities as Pittsburgh, Minneapolis, or St. Louis achieve such tremendous gains over the last few decades—when cities with apparently superior assets have remained "stuck" in old economy grooves? The answer to this question requires understanding the dynamic interplay between the development of a cluster of entrepreneurial research institutions and the growth of an entrepreneurial business development community facilitated by a unique technology commercialization initiative, UCSD CONNECT.

CONNECT is an organization that links promising research initiatives and technology business developers with the capital resources and entrepreneurial business know-how needed for success (see www.connect.org/). It has facilitated the development of hundreds of successful technology companies in San Diego. With a small staff that organizes dozens of savvy volunteer committees and hundreds of individual presenters, reviewers, and mentors, CONNECT annually offers close to one hundred events, forums, roundtables, and workshops, which effectively "connect" all the partners needed to start and grow a business. Two signature programs include Springboard, which offers free assistance to life science and high-tech companies in all stages of development;

and Global CONNECT, a collection of organizations and firms, regional development organizations, university programs, and capital service providers from more than forty regions around the world working together to develop international high-technology and life science linkages. Members are vital to the financial health of the organization, are key partners in the delivery of quality programming, and participation in committees and programs is instrumental in enabling the organization to offer its variety of programs and services. There were 150 members in 2006 distributed as follows: professional and strategic (45 percent), industry (30 percent), capital providers (15 percent), and research affiliates (10 percent).

REQUIREMENTS FOR TRANSFORMING DISCOVERY INTO A VIABLE BUSINESS

The journey from a promising idea or finding into a useful technology that solves a real problem in a manner that is scalable, affordable, and marketable is what technology commercialization is about. It goes beyond issues of patenting and knowledge transfer and focuses squarely on testing, demonstrating, validating, and ultimately translating a promising idea into a useful and marketable product. It is a journey that Duane Roth, the current CEO of CONNECT, describes as the "four Ds": discovery research, defining a potential application, developing and validating the application, and delivering the solution to a market. For this to occur, a number of conditions are necessary and a variety of competencies are essential, all of which are captured by the CONNECT model developed through trial and error at UCSD in the 1980s. An active focus on technology commercialization similar to that enabled by the UCSD CONNECT model can result in the rapid growth of robust science-based company clusters such as those established in IT, life science, and software in San Diego in recent decades. These clusters of companies have created tens of thousands of high-wage jobs, new tax revenues, and personal wealth, which combined have been a powerful driver of regional economic development.

Effective commercialization systems are enabled by five critical elements:

1. Cross-professional knowledge relevant to innovation in the technology and business communities:

   a. Tech-savvy business community
   b. Business-savvy science community

2. An experimental, risk-oriented culture adept at managing uncertainty in the technology and business communities:

   a. Discovery, experimental, risky science; entrepreneurial and risk-savvy science
   b. Nimble business culture and practices; entrepreneurial business know-how

3. Platforms through which these two communities connect. This means integrative mechanisms that enable frequent pretransactional communication, resulting in increased trust and a shared sense of purpose.

4. The presence of honest brokers and multiple gateways to increase frequency and diversity of interaction. These enable knowledge flow and trust building, leading to faster, increased application and commercialization activities that will create more proven products, successful companies, new jobs, and new wealth.

5. A culture of reinvestment—successful entrepreneurs as well as entrepreneurial teams share their "know-how" and support others by:

   - Sharing knowledge and relationships
   - Contributing time
   - Investing personal cash in new ventures
   - Providing access to capital for promising ventures
   - Contributing to regional institutions through philanthropy
   - Seeking a return on involvement, through meaningful tasks with visible outcomes that benefit the region as well as themselves

Each of these elements deserves further description with specific examples from UCSD CONNECT activities.

Components of the UCSD CONNECT Program

Cross-Professional Knowledge Relevant to Innovation

The University of California campus in San Diego was established in the late 1950s and opened its doors to PhD students in 1960. The growth strategy was to build a cadre of senior-level faculty across a number of academic disciplines in order to attract the best and the brightest and quickly build a research university. The faculty in the early years brought with them significant research grants and was a magnet for excellent graduate students and postdocs, so that by the time the campus opened its doors to freshmen it already had a small but distinguished, well-funded research faculty in place. This faculty was made up of basic scientists who had minimal interest in industrial relations or technology commercialization. A small number of the early faculty members, however, were involved in research areas that had promising applications in the solution of real-world problems. Notable among these were:

- Irwin Jacobs, professor of electrical engineering and computer science, who consulted with the U.S. Navy on remote signal processing, and refined the CDMA technology platform that became the basis for the founding of the company Linkabit in the early 1970s and of Qualcomm in the mid 1980s.
- Ivor Royston, professor of medicine, who worked in the groundbreaking field of monoclonal antibodies in cancer research, and founded a company, Hybritech, in the early 1970s, in large part because he needed cell samples for his research lab.

The success of Linkabit and Hybritech less than twenty years after the founding of the university created a buzz in the San Diego region that led people to believe it might be possible to grow robust clusters of high-technology companies on the model of Silicon Valley.

Simultaneous with the growth of the UCSD campus and these early company successes that built upon the entrepreneurial energies of two professors came a recession in California and in San

Diego that had profound and troubling effects. A combination of factors—the savings and loan crisis of the early 1980s; the increasing competitiveness of European and Asian nations in R&D; shifting investments by the Department of Defense; and the unsuccessful attempts in the early 1980s to attract major companies or research consortia to the region, led by the San Diego Regional Economic Corporation—led to high unemployment in San Diego and a deep concern about where its economic future would lie. As a result, civic leaders, who were not especially sophisticated about science and technology, but were aware of some of the early individual company successes associated with the young University of California campus, asked Chancellor Richard C. Atkinson how the campus might become more of a partner in regional economic development. Atkinson had been a professor at Stanford for more than twenty years and had just come from six years as director of the National Science Foundation. He had worked closely with Senators Birch Bayh and Robert Dole to develop the legislation that enabled the commercialization of federally funded research. He was highly responsive to these community overtures and dispatched a small group of university colleagues to investigate what might be possible.

I had just been appointed dean of the university's extension service and, as a research sociologist, had been doing interviews in the Silicon Valley to understand the dynamics of innovation in that region. Based on knowledge of the dynamics of Silicon Valley and interviews with key supporters in San Diego, we prepared a brief report for the chancellor and a few key stakeholders describing what the community needed to build on the successes of early start-up companies such as Linkabit and Hybritech in order to grow robust clusters of science and technology companies similar to those in the Silicon Valley.

It was at this time that the core concept of the CONNECT program emerged. When the scientists and engineers that started successful companies were interviewed, their primary emphasis was on the need for a more responsive, nimble, and technology-savvy business community. In the late 1970s and early 1980s, engineers and scientists who became company entrepreneurs secured their funding, and their legal, accounting, and marketing services, outside San Diego because of the absence of a professional business service community capable of responding to their distinctive needs. Of particular note was the need for service providers with some understanding of technology, intellectual property, and the risk cycles involved with start-ups, as well as a knowledge of global regulatory and marketing challenges. San Diego had been a community characterized by tourism, agriculture, and defense contracting and therefore lacked a business community capable of working with the entrepreneurial scientists who were aggregating around the UCSD campus and the other research institutions on the Torrey Pines Mesa, such as the Scripps Research Institute and the Salk Institute.

In contrast, when local business leaders were asked about what they felt would be needed to grow robust science-based clusters, predictably they emphasized the need for scientists and engineers to become more sophisticated about the real costs of producing particular technology solutions, developing a clearer sense of the market for their technologies and increasing their willingness to work with more professional managers in realizing the potential of their technology, particularly through a profitable business. In other words, they needed business skills.

These two contrasting views of pressing needs actually became two interlocking themes in all of the developments within UCSD CONNECT over the next twenty years. Everyone today recognizes that innovations in science and technology are supported by an ecosystem of complementary competencies and resources. What was distinctive about the CONNECT program in the 1980s was that in mirroring the success of Silicon Valley, it was set up to become the hub or connective link within that ecosystem of innovation for the San Diego region. In its mission and goals, represented in a one-page statement, its founding members and its early programs reflected these two themes: the need to develop more science and technology product development sophistication among the business community, and more financial, marketing and management intelligence among the scientific community. Through more than eighty programs annually, focused on themes such as "Meet the Researcher" for businesspeople and "Global Strategies for Financing High-Tech Companies" for scientists and engineers, the CONNECT program was able to build the cross-professional knowledge networks essential for innovation.

A RISK-ORIENTED CULTURE ADEPT AT MANAGING UNCERTAINTY

The commercialization support efforts of the CONNECT program resulted in large numbers of companies securing venture capital and three times as many CONNECT-assisted companies were still in business five years after receiving CONNECT support, as compared to other start-ups. This was helped by the rapidity with which the business community came to understand and respect the wide range of "risky" cutting-edge research initiatives taking place on the Torrey Pines Mesa and the extent to which the scientists, because of their interaction on a regular basis with the business community, began to respect the competencies and resources that the business community could bring to the commercialization enterprise.

The character of the research institutions across the Torrey Pines Mesa, not just the UCSD campus, was shaped in the 1960s and 1970s by a culture of excellence. The recruitment strategies for faculty and researchers focused on bringing people who were at the "front end" of knowledge development and involved in highly interdisciplinary endeavors. The result was a significant infusion of federal and foundation dollars in a short time to the institutions across the Mesa and a growing identity of the region as involved in "breakthrough" science. It is important to understand the extent to which one must be tenacious and entrepreneurial to secure the level of funding that the scientists across the Torrey Pines Mesa were able to secure then and now. This is an entrepreneurial skill that not all research scientists at all research universities possess; it may be one of the differentiating characteristics of the scientists at the highest-performing research institutions. The business community understood early on that this was an unusual set of skills and they developed a respect for this kind of science. It helped that many of the early companies, though not direct spin-offs from UCSD or Salk, involved faculty and researchers working in those institutions. It also was a result of the articulate leadership of Richard C. Atkinson and the breadth of programs sponsored by UCSD CONNECT that celebrated good science and fundamental research.

At the same time, the business community, including law, accounting, and marketing firms and even real estate developers, was developing more sophisticated entrepreneurial skills and relationships. Within a decade of the founding of CONNECT, dozens of law firms in the region formed strategic partnerships with IP law firms from other parts of the country. The various venture forums sponsored by CONNECT in its early years resulted in many venture funds establishing offices in the San Diego region. A number of national marketing firms with technology clients and experience in global markets opened offices or formed strategic alliances with local marketing firms. Within a decade, a genuinely risk-oriented culture adept at managing the uncertainties involved in managing R&D start-ups became firmly established in the region. By the mid-1990s, growth in company formations, venture capital funding, and IPOs was almost exponential.

INTEGRATIVE PLATFORMS

A fundamental concept in sociology is that frequent interaction between people and groups increases understanding and affection. George Homans, a leading theoretical sociologist at Harvard University, asserted this sociological principle decades ago and empirical evidence supports it. UCSD CONNECT represents an integrative mechanism, a platform for activities that increases interactions between previously isolated communities. If innovation occurs in an ecosystem, a community needs a place where diverse interests, knowledge bases, and resources can connect. This ecosystem evolved slowly in Silicon Valley and along the Route 128 corridor in Massachusetts. Since the 1980s, however, it has been enabled and facilitated by university aligned or located programs such as IC^2 at the University of Texas, Austin, the Council for Entrepreneurial Development in the North Carolina Research Triangle Park, and UCSD CONNECT on the Torrey Pines Mesa in La Jolla.

These platforms represent more than just a collection of networking activities and events. They involve stakeholders in a variety of meaningful interactions that produce three sets of benefits:

a. They organize activities that harvest experience and knowledge in the region in a manner that can truly help the scientist seeking validation for an idea or the entrepreneur seeking input on a business plan.

b. They occur in a setting that is pretransactional and completely open. Ideas and plans can be discussed, criticized, and adapted in a highly collegial manner in advance of an "official" presentation for angel capital, the development of a business plan for venture capital or corporate partnering. To this end, a culture emerges in which ideas are not stolen and side deals are not made and, as a consequence, people feel free to share their knowledge in an open and collegial manner.

c. The nature of the interaction is such that people learn not only about specific technologies or business plans, but about one another. That is how a community of innovation and a culture of shared risk can evolve. In surveying members who contribute endless hours to various CONNECT mentoring, evaluation, and education programs, one hears again and again that, "I participate in these programs as much for what I learn about my colleagues as because of the exposure to new ideas and new business plans. Getting familiar with the 'personalities' as well as the capabilities and client lists of my peers in the business community helps me put together teams in the future that work for the companies I'm supporting." The events and activities sponsored by a commercializing platform need to have these key characteristics.

The upshot is an enormous amount of information and resource sharing among a large community. The comment one often hears at various CONNECT events is, "I can't personally help you but I have a friend or a colleague who's very good at this." Or, "There's no one in San Diego who's working in this particular space but I have a good friend in Seattle who is supporting a company of this nature. Let me get his name to you immediately." This spirit of not just knowledge sharing but resource and relationship sharing is absolutely critical in connecting the two communities.

Finally, on many occasions, scientists and engineers navigating through the various CONNECT programs to explore the potential for commercialization of an idea or application have not yet resolved whether they should try to patent or license their technology. The close interactions between CONNECT and the technology transfer offices from the various research institutions on the Torrey Pines Mesa help mitigate the potential dangers of sharing an idea before it is patented. The other benefit of the platform is that it becomes a receptor community for many of the promising patents and licensing arrangements coming out of the various technology transfer offices across the research institutions on the Mesa. Protection of intellectual property is absolutely critical once an idea or application is defined as having real promise. The journey through the testing and validation of the idea or application and the exploration of its viability in terms of production, marketing, and pricing, however, is the longer journey in the commercialization process for which the CONNECT platform has proved so valuable. It is for this reason that traditional technology transfer offices work so closely and effectively with the CONNECT program.

MULTIPLE GATEWAYS

Above and beyond the existence of the CONNECT program as an integrative platform that draws in the knowledge and resources of both the entrepreneurial science community and the entrepreneurial business community, there is enormous value in having multiple gateways through which science and business can interact. UCSD CONNECT learned early on that it did not need to be the gatekeeper, the central door through which all industry interactions including tech transfer occurred, but rather it could be one of many honest brokers in the ecosystem. Once again, recent research bears out the value of multiple points of entry in a knowledge-creating community. The frequency and diversity of interactions through industrial affiliate programs, technology commercialization initiatives, entrepreneurship education in schools of engineering, and nimble offices of technology transfer result in knowledge flowing in many directions, leading to faster and more effective application, development, and commercialization of promising research initiatives. Universities such as UC San Diego and Stanford have dozens of offices located in multiple departments and schools through which industry interactions occur. These represent an important part of the innovation equation because the ease with which people can have access to the knowledge that ultimately produces products, companies, jobs, and wealth can accelerate the rate of start-ups.

The UCSD example is instructive. CONNECT was founded before there was an office of technology transfer at UCSD and simultaneous with the establishment of the first industrial affiliates program at UCSD. At the time CONNECT was founded there were no technology industry groups in the San Diego region except for the American Electronics Association whose members were engineers drawn primarily from defense contracting businesses. CONNECT in its first decade became the platform through which a variety of campus-based industrial affiliates programs were formed and a number of industry specific advocacy groups were spun off, in particular BIOCOM and the Regional Technology Alliance. CONNECT has been a strategic partner in the development of the von Liebig Center for Entrepreneurial Studies within the School of Engineering, the clinical research initiatives in the School of Medicine, and a variety of other independent but aligned activities.

Multiple gateways matter. A commercialization platform is critical but it is also essential to engage all of the various paths to knowledge development and technology connections. The CONNECT program differs from many other commercialization efforts throughout the United States and the world by being part of the ecosystem, not on top of it or the exclusive gateway to it. As such, it benefits enormously from lots of good ideas and business development opportunities flowing into its offices from multiple sources. The most recent data on high-tech company formation in San Diego indicate that a new high-tech company is started every seventeen hours. This is a sign that the highly fluid ecosystem of innovation is working effectively.

A Culture of Reinvestment

A final characteristic of highly successful commercialization systems, and especially university-anchored programs such as

CONNECT, is the culture of reinvestment. Successful entrepreneurs, whether they are scientists or businesspeople, and the teams they develop, share their know-how, support others that are attempting to replicate their efforts or success, and make a commitment to growing the innovation culture of which they are a part. Based on the extraordinary involvement of literally hundreds of scientists and businesspeople from the San Diego region in the various programs of CONNECT, it is possible to describe the ways in which this culture of reinvestment expresses itself.

It begins with a sharing of knowledge and relationships that can be mobilized to support the work of relatively unknown and untried individuals and ideas. Through mentoring, seminars, workshops, and interactive roundtables, more experienced professionals and scientists share their knowledge with less experienced people and are generous in their efforts to help make connections that contribute to success. This type of sharing involves significant contributions of personal time by a wide range of individuals. In CONNECT's case, these individuals are not simply successful entrepreneurs with discretionary time and money to mentor and support new business ventures. Participants include large numbers of well-educated, highly seasoned professionals whose typical billable hour represents hundreds of dollars. Through the CONNECT program these individuals contribute their time, wisdom, and experience on a pro bono basis.

Reinvestment also involves cash. CONNECT was the incubator for the formation of an angel investment group known as the Tech Coast Angels that today numbers more than 140 individuals. Using the offices of CONNECT and sharing support staff, the Tech Coast Angels meet at the University Faculty Club once a month for briefings on exciting new developments in which angel investment could make a difference. This group includes a wide array of individuals with diverse business backgrounds (retired attorneys and bankers, successful real estate developers, and savvy tech entrepreneurs). Just as important as the involvement of early-stage angel investors in the commercialization process is access to institutional sources of capital, such as venture capital and corporate partnering. Successful entrepreneurs and experienced, well-connected business service providers in the region are often bridges to major sources of capital for new companies. Through these individuals, doors are constantly opening for the young, the unknown, or a spin-off team from an established company.

Finally, one of the most interesting things about the San Diego area and the role of UCSD CONNECT in the region is the extraordinary growth in philanthropy over the last thirty years. The vast majority of new philanthropic funds are in personal foundations, family foundations, and mechanisms such as community foundations and the Jewish Family Foundation, which have come from the wealth created by successful science and technology entrepreneurs in the region. Hundreds of millions of dollars in new funds have been established and much has been contributed to the university in the form of endowed chairs, fellowships, and financial support for promising graduate students as well as for buildings and physical facilities. CONNECT often acts as a partner in the development of these resources and played a leadership role in the growth of endowed chairs at the university, the establishment of a new graduate school of business at the university, in the formation of a collaborative for regenerative medicine involving all the research institutions on the Torrey Pines Mesa, as well as in supporting K–12 charter schools focused on developing the pipeline of math-and-science talent pool. This spirit of philanthropy and culture of reinvestment has been critical for the university's continued success as a leading research institution as well as the growth of robust clusters of innovative science-based companies in the San Diego region.

Surveys of the pro bono participants and investors in many of the CONNECT activities reveal that people are looking for two kinds of return on investment. Clearly business development is one of the things that motivate participation; however, as important as financial return is the return on involvement and participation. Because the commercialization strategies developed by CONNECT involve meaningful tasks with visible outcomes that benefit the region as well as the individual participants, there is a sense of contributing to civic well-being by being a part of the CONNECT network. CONNECT's efforts are clearly enhanced by the membership fees and program underwriting support so generously provided by a variety of businesses across the region, but it is also the personal involvement by hundreds of professionals and scientists that makes the CONNECT program work. Annually, the CONNECT program sponsors more than eighty different events and activities and secures program fees, membership fees, underwriting, and philanthropy that approaches $2 million in private sector support. It receives no university funding for any of its staff or activities nor does it receive city, county, or state funding. It is a fully self-supporting, community-engaging technology commercialization initiative characterized by a strong culture of reinvestment.

Concluding Observations on UCSD CONNECT

Universities need to become more actively engaged in technology commercialization in order to fulfill their responsibility to be vital partners in regional economic growth and transformation. The strong role of Stanford University in Silicon Valley is an excellent example of how multiple relationships between the business community and a variety of academic programs, departments, and schools increase the ability of knowledge to be transferred and support to be provided in the commercialization of promising ideas. The case of UCSD CONNECT is instructive because it built on the experiences of early innovators such as Stanford and, after listening to key stakeholders, developed an integrative platform that ensured frequent and meaningful interactions among researchers, entrepreneurs, and business service providers. A cocreation of the university and business leaders, the program has been for more than twenty years a kind of "incubator without walls" for UCSD and for the entire Torrey Pines Mesa. As of 2005, CONNECT became an independent 501(c)3 organization, in order to more broadly serve the full array of basic research institutions on the Torrey Pines Mesa. Without the reputational and in-kind institutional support provided by UCSD in its first twenty years, it might not have become the sustainable organization it is today.

San Diego, which was home to a mere handful of science-based companies thirty years ago, is a global leader today in aggregated annual research funding as well as in the size and robustness of its science-based clusters, particularly in the life sciences, IT, and software. UCSD CONNECT has been critical in this transformation. This is because technology commercialization is a journey requiring multiple steps and relationships characterized by incremental milestones and frequent setbacks. It is an interactive, adaptive process—not a one-time transaction. The identification and definition of a promising application, the testing and development of that application through proof of concept work or clinical trials, and the ultimate delivery of the application to receptive users all require at every step knowledge and resources beyond those available in a researchers' laboratory. This is what programs such as UCSD CONNECT provide. The orchestrated activities enabled by the CONNECT platform are extremely helpful in developing an entrepreneurial culture and in building robust clusters of technology companies that benefit regional economies.

CHAPTER TEN

NINE PRINCIPLES FOR SUCCESSFUL UNIVERSITY-INDUSTRY RELATIONS

Robert C. Miller and Bernard J. Le Boeuf

The chapters in this book describe offices and operations that have made knowledge transfer work well. They have in common a set of principles that govern their work.

Build relationships and enhance goodwill. The emphasis is not solely on making money from a particular operation such as exclusive licensing of patents, but on increasing the impact of university research.

Extend the teaching mission of the university by deploying technologies developed in the course of university research into the private sector. Technology transfer is not just about research but also is a quintessential *teaching* mission. This means teaching the university-developed technologies to companies through agreements and by the employment of graduate students.

Encourage and develop entrepreneurs in the university. This involves providing user-friendly mechanisms for students and faculty to work in a wide range of university-company environments. It also involves building new courses on topics such as starting a software company.

Ensure that both faculty and students are knowledgeable and comfortable with any negotiated agreement. The first key to any successful technology transfer project is to ensure the continuing positive involvement of the contributing faculty and students. There was a time when tech transfer operations were built on the theory that faculty disclosed inventions and then were left behind as professionals patented and licensed the technologies disclosed. This process originally generated some large single technology revenue streams which now have decreased significantly as a fraction of the revenue generated from university-industry agreements. But just as the economy has changed over the years, faculty and students have become more sophisticated and entrepreneurial.

Communicate the objectives of the university, faculty, and students early in discussions with prospective company partners. Universities have limitations on the terms of agreements which are acceptable under policy, regulations, and laws. These limitations should be clear at the beginning of any discussion. Negotiations between companies and universities frequently are bogged down in misunderstanding over these limitations and other unrealistic expectations held by all parties. Consequently, a window of opportunity passes before agreement based on realistic terms can be achieved.

Make the mission of industry liaison–tech transfer clear and provide appropriate resources. All too frequently the expectations for the relevant offices are not clear, and a drive for licensing revenue as the prime funding source drags down university-industry affairs in general. University-industry agreements demand management by knowledgeable professionals with significant expertise. A university should emphasize training, recruitment, and retention of these people.

Develop metrics of success that reflect all aspects of university-industry affairs. The total revenue coming to the university includes the direct and indirect costs of research, exclusive and nonexclusive licensing fees, reimbursement of patent costs, equity in start-up companies, funds from leased lands or buildings to operations designed to support start-up companies, service contracts for use of specialized equipment, graduate fellowships, and philanthropic donations. Too much emphasis or incentives toward monetary returns from licensing patents can jeopardize all the other funds and support from industry. Metrics of success should reflect the sum of these activities.

Support an integrated approach to the management of university-industry affairs. It is essential to install a knowledgeable, senior academic administrator to coordinate all the agreements with companies so that no relationship is jeopardized by neglect or ambiguity in authority of the university office in charge of a particular agreement.

Economic development should be viewed realistically and valued as a role for the university. Michael E. Porter's concept of clusters emphasizes the essential role of research universities in local clusters of high-tech industry. But this assertion should not be extended to the point that universities are seen to drive the economy. Programs such as UCSD CONNECT, the graduation of a knowledgeable, entrepreneurial workforce, and productive research relationships are likely to have the most effect in this arena.

The take-home message to university administrators and CEOs is as follows. Great universities and strong industry involvement have a tremendous track record of excellence. University leaders are advised to build across a range of innovation enterprises to engage the community. Do not leave patent management to a solitary unit tasked with making windfall money. Bayh-Dole is about giving universities the chance to be leaders in technology innovation; that is the role for a broad range of publicly funded research and no one should avoid it. Build new programs of almost any kind and create the points of engagement that stimulate excellence.

Glossary of Terms

Gerald Barnett

This field guide to terms of art in research technology administration is intended to give the reader a sense of the range of usage of common words as well as an idea of the more esoteric ones.

Agreement

An agreement is a mutual understanding with regard to a given topic. Agreements may be recorded in contracts, but do not have to be. In research settings there may be any number of agreements that are not contractual. Company scientists and university scientists may agree to organize a conference, or to pursue a particular line of research, or to seek federal funding for a project of mutual interest. Such agreements may be documented by e-mail exchanges or meeting notes, but do not rise to the level of contracts. However, such agreements may create a sense of social obligation or concern for reputation. In any intellectual property agreement, there are typically five fundamental elements at stake—ownership, control, money, attribution, and risk. As an agreement is promoted to the status of an institutional obligation, it tends to become a contract. Institutional agreements that are not contracts are called "relationships" and may be documented by memoranda of understanding, exchange of written communication, or by repeated patterns of dealing.

Angel investor

An angel is a private investor who participates in start-up activities by contributing personal funds, often under $250,000, and working with entrepreneurs. Angel investors may work together in groups, such as the Sand Hill Angels in Palo Alto, California, or may work on their own. Angel investors are usually located close to home, taking an interest in opportunities within a fifty-mile radius. Angel investments are often called "pre-seed" or "seed" round investments, to be distinguished from a substantial first round of equity investment.

Bayh-Dole Act

The Bayh-Dole Act is a U.S. federal law passed in 1980 to harmonize federal agency invention management in extramural contracts with small businesses, universities, and other nonprofit research organizations. The Bayh-Dole Act encourages use of the U.S. patent system to bring federally funded inventions to practical application for the benefit of the public, to build relationships between universities and industry, and to support the participation of U.S. small businesses in the development of federal inventions. Under Bayh-Dole, universities may elect title in federally funded inventions, provided that they file patent applications and seek to license rights for commercial uses. There is no obligation requiring payment for such licenses, but any such income must be shared with the inventors, and revenue remaining after costs is to be used for scientific research and education.

Community-connect programs

Outreach programs provide access and services to populations that often do not participate in government or community programs. University programs that engage in this way include extension (instruction), agricultural extension (farm service), and various sports and arts programs. Research-oriented connect programs often emphasize entrepreneurship, innovation, and venture investment.

Company incubation

A company incubator is a cluster of resources, often located in a multitenant facility, that provides a variety of services in support of early-stage companies. These services may include access to photocopy and communications equipment, secretarial support, specialized research labs, and connections with professional services such as management guidance, law, accounting, and investment. Incubators are challenged in how they recruit companies, how these companies pay their way, and how companies "graduate" from the incubator to facilities that are not subsidized. Incubators may be operated by universities, communities, or through free-standing companies.

Contract

A contract is an agreement characterized by offer, acceptance, and consideration, and is enforceable on the parties involved. A contract may be oral or written, and may be stated directly (express) or implied (as by actions). A grant of funding may be made by gift or by contract. Similarly, a license may be granted without a contract (in which case, it may be rescinded) or by means of a contract. In the context of a license, it is the recipient of the license—the licensee—that usually desires a license contract, so the permission granted is firm. The licensor may require a contract to ensure payment and proper handling of rights and technology transferred to the licensee.

Cross-collateralization

Cross-collateralization is a way of spreading risk across a set of relationships. Collateral for one loan is used as security for other loans. This is also known as *joint accounting*, linking the income from one asset to repayment of debt for another.

Disclosures

A disclosure in technology transfer is a report of a new invention, typically on a form provided by the employer or sponsor. Disclosure documents vary greatly among institutions, but share a common emphasis on documenting a new invention, the inventors, and funding sources that may create obligations for handling. Disclosure forms may also request information about the history of the inventive work, possible markets for the invention, planned improvements, and the like. Disclosure is often used synonymously with "invention" or "case" or "technology," but in fact disclosures are tremendously varied. A single document may record multiple inventions, leading to a number of patents. Similarly, a technology can be broken up into multiple disclosures, each recording a "least reportable element" which during the patent application process are combined into fewer claimed inventions.

Thus, in general, there is not a one-to-one relationship between disclosures and inventions, or inventions and patents.

Facilities and administrative rate (F&A)

The F&A is an estimate of the full cost of conducting a research project, typically one supported by an external sponsor. It is otherwise known as the "indirect cost" rate, or "burden" in federal circles. F&A covers costs that otherwise are difficult to direct bill against any single project—electricity, maintenance, and janitorial services for research facilities, administrative support to manage the systems that provide oversight, compliance, and reporting on research projects.

The U.S. Government has a mandate to provide full cost recovery for work supported at universities. Universities therefore break up their research budgets to include direct costs, plus an amount for facilities and administration as a percentage of modified direct costs. The rate for each university is set through negotiation with an agency designated by the federal government as the primary contact for that university. The government requires that it receive the best indirect cost rate offered to any sponsor. The range of university indirect costs rates is between 35 percent and 75 percent of direct costs. While the government's arrangements with industry contractors are not generally available, industry indirect rates for research are often 100–130 percent.

Industry and private foundations have no mandate to provide full cost recovery and frequently seek ways to avoid indirect cost charges. Often they are supported by faculty investigators who see the F&A as a take-away from their own projects. One end run involves providing research funding as a gift, which typically is charged a much lower gift administration fee (often around 5 percent). Another is to offer "joint study" opportunities in which each party pays its own way, but provides access to resources needed by the other. Because such arrangements may exchange value (a company might waive facilities fees rather than pay the university to acquire its own equipment) but do not result in the creation of a direct budget with cash changing hands, there is no F&A as a percentage of direct charges. There are more sophisticated end runs to indirect costs. One way is to develop an affiliates membership program. Another way is charging a licensing fee for copyright materials and using these fees for further work. Yet another way is to provide a modest grant of funds carrying F&A combined with a parallel cash donation to the same lab, such as a fellowship.

F&A is divided into revenue pools and parceled out within the university. The processes for doing so are often tightly guarded and not reported broadly in the university. Technology transfer offices typically do not participate in F&A pools, even though the disclosure and reporting function of their offices, as well as the negotiation of IP, data, and publishing clauses in research agreements are directly tied to sponsored project administration.

Industry consortia

A consortium is a research structure consisting of a number of organizations collaborating in the conduct of work, sharing of expenses, and management of results. The National Science Foundation Industry/University Cooperative Research Center (I/UCRC) program has created over fifty such consortia, nearly all of which are now focused on engineering-based work. I/UCRC consortia receive annual government funding on the condition that the funds are matched by industry members. Consortia are usually governed by a university-based consortium director and an industry advisory board (IAB) representing the company members. Collaborative research conducted by a consortium may solve industry problems but more frequently provides training for graduate students and industry scientists in current technology.

Management overhead for consortia can be quite high. Once government support ends, consortia often wind down and reform around new initiatives. Substantial effort is needed to recruit industry members, negotiate a standard membership agreement, and deal with competing interests involving intellectual property, publication, and risk. Apparently simple matters such as when industry members join or leave can be complicated by issues such as access to technology licenses, management of "back taxes" for joining later than others, and the like.

Intellectual property (IP)

Intellectual property is a form of intangible asset recognized by law as protectable as to ownership. The classic forms of intellectual property are patents, copyrights, and trademarks. Trade secret is sometimes included with intellectual property, but arises not from statute but from contracts that prevent disclosure. New forms of intangible asset, such as Internet domain names, have many properties of intellectual property. The World Intellectual Property Organization proposes that traditional knowledge may also form a class of intellectual property, though generally not recognized by national statutes. One may observe that university investigators have much in common with other informal populations less interested in statutory formalities and more given to advancing academic practices.

Intellectual property arises in research settings across a wide range of assets and activities. In addition to breakthrough inventions and discoveries, patents can also be obtained for research tools and methods. Copyrights attach to software, data sets, technical reports, images and diagrams, simulations and models, and collections of information. Trademark rights may arise through use in the names and logos of research laboratories and centers, software and biomaterials, as well as specific models and particular research services. Although those intellectual property rights that have the potential to be significant either as community-changing discoveries or wealth-creating engines are relatively few—perhaps fewer than one in two thousand invention reports—research activities generate a tremendous number of potential claims to ownership.

Intellectual property can be thought of as a set of innovations to manage competitive pressures, especially among organizations, and to establish a degree of control over assets by authors and inventors in their dealings with others. Seen in this light, patents and copyrights, and the much more ancient trademarks, can play an important role in establishing the degree of respect a community owes to innovators. While it is natural—especially for powerful organizations or talented performers—to want to take whatever they find, intellectual property proposes a shift in balance in favor of those doing the discovering. Such a shift leads to a more favorable climate for publication over secrecy, the creation of investment marketplaces over domination by the most powerful, and a return to discoverers and writers even when these individuals and organizations are not themselves suited to the task of development or distribution. While the balance of rights and respect is not always perfect for given areas of developing practice, the overall thrust of adding intellectual property to an innovation system is to provide a driver for independent initiative. Though one can imagine perfect societies in which innovation is rewarded openly and freely, in point of practice in the societies we have, this does not happen so often that one can be faulted for desiring an intellectual property handle to manage one's bit of contribution to the common good—especially as this may be mediated through a manufacturer's or publisher's more immediate, and tangible, financial benefit.

Invention

"Invention" has popular and technical definitions. Popularly, an invention is any clever new thing that does something useful. For patent purposes, in addition to being new and useful, an invention must also be "non-obvious." An invention is made when it is both "conceived" and "reduced to practice." Conception is the mental activity of realizing the nature of the invention, how to make it, and what functions it performs. Reduction to practice is broader—it can mean constructing and testing the invention to demonstrate its efficacy, or it can mean filing a patent application, regardless of whether the invention has been constructed. This division of conception and reduction to practice leads to challenges in research invention management. Bayh-Dole claims federal interest in any invention that is conceived or reduced to practice if funded in whole or in part through federal funding. One could have the idea for an invention, and work to develop it with federal funding, bringing the patent rights within the scope of federal claims. Or one could conceive of the invention while working on a federal grant, and develop it subsequently with private support.

License

A license gives permission to practice under rights held by the grantor of the license. Licensing is at the heart of a great irony in university research management. Intellectual property is a negative right. The owner of a patent has the right, under the law, to exclude others from making, using, or selling products that come within the claims of the patent. A license is therefore a promise not to assert the rights one has under the patent law. A similar situation exists for copyright. Why do this? If a primary goal of technology transfer is to move research results into practical application, why work to obtain the right to exclude others? Holding intellectual property appears to run against the goal. Why not just leave things alone and let everyone do what they want with the research? This irony is not lost on companies working with research universities.

A common rationale for taking ownership in order to grant licenses is that an exclusive position provides a commercial partner with an incentive to invest in a research technology. Other arguments include quality control, integrity of reports or findings, choice of early associations for evaluation and development, creation of standards, and risk management. Technology-based economic development advocates face conflicting desires—on the one hand, they like research findings being readily available to entrepreneurs without an added step of dealing with a university licensing office. On the other hand, as entrepreneurs take findings out of the area, they see the value of establishing ownership positions if only to give local entrepreneurs an advantage in keeping valuable assets local.

Invariably, the focus on developing research for practical application or on encouraging local economic vitality through ready access to outcomes gives way to professional management that views the intellectual property rights as the primary assets. In this formulation, patent rights are a basis for income generation based on *getting there first* rather than on *helping others get there next*. Unfortunately, university royalty-sharing policies may create an expectation among researchers that the university has an obligation to generate income from licensing, to enforce contracts rather than restructure them to meet changing conditions, and to sue infringers (practical application!) where no licenses have been granted. All of this leads to a shift from the transfer of technology to a transfer, strictly, of rights in exchange for payment. To some extent, this confusion of operating models—technology transfer as premium and timely instruction in emerging research, and rights transfer as a monetizing of intellectual property positions based on the threat to block practice—leads to dissatisfaction in the research community, whether academic or corporate.

A license can be stated expressly in a contract, implied through a pattern of dealing, or included in a broader grant or other action. When there is intellectual property, it is the recipient of the license that most needs a contract, for it is the contract that prevents the licensor from withdrawing the license at any time. Since a contract requires consideration for the benefit granted to make it enforceable, it is also, technically, the recipient of the license that must feel the need to offer something of value. In technology transfer, the licensor views a contract as a means to require diligent development and as a way to revoke the license if this diligence is not met, or payment is not made. A contract can also spell out protocols for managing patent work, dealing with infringement, allocating responsibilities and risk, and handling disagreements.

Licensed technologies

A technology is a general placeholder for any invention, development, or research finding protectable as to ownership. Unlike a patent, which is a form of intellectual property, a technology is a body of practice, information, and tangible materials, together with any intellectual property and other rights (such as ownership of material items or chattels) that attach to exploitation of the practice, information, and materials. Transfer of a technology through licensing generally involves granting licenses in patent rights and copyrights along with delivery of information, materials, and instruction in how to use and practice the technology. Patent licensing may not involve any such delivery beyond the grant of license. However, copyright and trade secret licenses generally require some form of delivery of information, media, or master copy. Technology transfer defined most broadly is an enabling form of instruction in which the recipient gains the capability to practice what has been taught. Clearly, providing rights that otherwise would preclude practice is necessary. Just as essential, however, is that the recipient be able to practice what has been licensed.

It should be noted that a technology may be licensed but not transferred. For instance, a patent right may be granted, and the licensee may use that patent right to develop new technology that uses the patented invention, but extends to other functions.

A licensor is generally careful not to license technology but rather licenses rights.

Material transfer agreement (MTA)

Various materials may be created and exchanged in the course of research. In addition to intellectual property rights, these "tangible research properties" or TRP are also treated as material goods in their own right. A material transfer agreement is used as a contract to manage the transfer of material, identify any special conditions or hazards, and comply with regulations and laws. The most common MTA is the Uniform Biomaterial Transfer Agreement promoted by the National Institutes of Health to simplify transfers of materials among nonprofit institutions. Participating institutions sign a master agreement and then use a simple letter format to identify the material to be transferred and manage the risk, rights, and payment terms, if any, that cover the cost of the transfer.

Industry to university MTAs can be difficult because an industry source of materials may require "reach through" terms that claim ownership or financial interest in any research results arising through the use of the transferred material. These reach through terms may conflict with other grant funding conditions and may not be equitable relative to the nature of the use of the material. For instance, a material used as a control rather than as the object of study plays a markedly different role in the production of research results.

Memorandum of understanding (MOU)

A memorandum of understanding is a written document that records an agreement. A MOU may have the force of contract but usually operates to establish good faith efforts toward a particular goal without requiring the parties to achieve the goal. Alternatively, a MOU can be nonbinding but serve as a common basis for further discussions and provide a public expression of an agreement between two parties. A MOU may be used in situations such as framing up a future research relationship or identifying roles in an ongoing collaboration.

Multitenant facilities

These facilities are research buildings in which multiple companies or teams work independently but benefit from a common location and access to resources. Research parks and business incubators often operate multitenant facilities to encourage cross-collaboration, create visibility, and develop economies of scale, especially as relating to access to highly specialized resources such as wet labs, clean rooms, and supercomputing resources.

Patent

A patent covers inventions that are new, useful, and non-obvious. Inventions may be methods, systems, devices, new forms of matter, or articles of manufacture. The patent gives the owner the right to exclude others from making, using, selling, or importing covered inventions. A patent is obtained by submitting an application to a patent office, where it is reviewed by an examiner. The application teaches the invention, describes the best mode of practicing the invention, and lays out in a series of claims the patent's scope of control. The examiner reviews the application for technical requirements and may challenge the scope of claims based on a review of published art. The applicant has the opportunity to revise, explain, or argue for specific elements of the application, but is not permitted to add new information to the application without refiling. The exchanges between examiner and applicant are called the patent prosecution, and a public record of these exchanges is available, when a patent issues, and is called the file "wrapper." A patent has a term of twenty years from the date of application. In the United States, a patent is awarded to the first to invent; in most of the rest of the world, a patent goes to the first applicant to file. Publication of an invention before filing an application results in loss of patent rights in much of the world, but in the United States, an applicant has a year to file from date of first publication, public use, or offer for sale of an invention.

Risk transfer

It is a truism of licensing that when one transfers rights, one also allocates risk. Risk comes in a variety of forms, including issues surrounding title to intellectual property, undocumented prior licenses or other liens, infringement of rights, product liability, contractual disputes, commercial disputes and events that spill over to license relationships such as bankruptcy, risk of reputation if a deal does not work out (and sometimes if it does), risk of damage or harm arising from contract-based work, and opportunity costs associated with choice of transactions on which to focus attention.

Management of risk begins with a working knowledge of the contemplated transaction, choice of business partners, allocation of resources to meet the demands of negotiating the transaction, and more important, of maintaining supervision and communication as the transaction moves forward. Risk can be divided into objective hazards and subjective hazards. Objective hazards come with the territory. By undertaking research in a given area, a university may be the object of protests. Subjective hazards arise from a failure of observation, judgment, or execution. Even in apparently safe settings, such failures can create substantial liability.

A risk that frequently arises for public universities in particular is the risk that a transaction cannot be completed in a timely manner, or completed at all, because of the overhead of various regulatory requirements.

Universities use external research foundations, holding companies, and patent management organizations to manage various kinds of risks that attend to research, licensing, and university-industry relationships. These external organizations take on university risk as an objective hazard and develop specialized resources to manage obligations to achieve results desired by their university partners and in line with public policy. This form of risk transfer enables a range of transactions, such as those involving private investment in real estate or developing technology, that a university could not directly manage as well, if at all.

Royalty income

Any consideration for the grant of a patent is technically a royalty. However, in practice "royalty" has three somewhat related uses. A royalty may be computed as a percentage of the income or an amount due for the sale of each unit of a licensed technology. In such cases it may also be called a "running royalty." When a company requests a "royalty free nonexclusive license," it may be willing to pay a one-time fee but wishes to avoid accounting for sales transactions in the future. Royalty payments may also be linked to cost savings and other measures of utility or benefit, though these are often difficult to track or enforce. A royalty may also be thought of a windfall payment received by a licensor. Thus, universities have "royalty sharing" policies that provide schedules governing how revenue paid by a licensee is to be divided among various parties in the university. Royalty income is typically distinguished from sponsored research funding, gift funding, and income from direct sales. Reimbursements for university patenting expenses may be treated as royalty income for purposes of reporting licensing income, but may not be considered royalty income to be shared under university policy. Materials transferred under an MTA may be subject to royalty sharing policies and may be treated under a different policy regarding revenue generation through sales. Equity realized from start-up companies may or may not be treated as royalty income, depending on the basis for the receipt of the equity interest.

Spin-off companies

A spin-off company is a start-up created to develop assets and market opportunities related to a larger project or initiative within a company or university. A university spin-off company typically seeks to develop a commercial product, but also may serve as a basis for provision of consulting services. In a company setting, a spin-off company may take out technology that is unrelated to the host company's present and future business directions. Technology that remains undeveloped at a host company is often referred to as "orphan" technology. Entrepreneurship in residence programs often target such orphan technology assets for possible new business opportunities.

A spin-off company may also be used synonymously with "start-up" company or "new co" in the context of moving research findings into commercial venues.

Sponsored research

Sponsored research is a concept that has arisen first in universities to account for foundation-based support for research projects undertaken by university investigators. As the federal government developed the National Science Foundation and similar health-related institutes as a primary vehicle for federal support for university research, the concept of sponsored research was formalized and adapted to allow university investigators to compete for federal research opportunities. Generally, a sponsored project consists of a proposal and budget, which, if approved by the external sponsor, is then combined with a research contract to memorialize the funding agreement. The concept of sponsored research and implementing university practices and policies is generally poorly suited to industry-university collaborations. Universities, however, have been loath to explore alternatives.

Sponsored-research contracting is typically handled through a university's office of sponsored projects, which manages the host of pre-award application requirements, negotiation of contracts, and post-award documentation, authorization of accounts, and management of the contractual research relationship.

Gift income from industry is generally not construed as sponsored research, even though funds may be used in an identical way within the university. Similarly, the receipt of materials and equipment from external sources may be construed as sponsored research, but more often this is considered to be either a donation (and received by the development office) or a form of business contract managed outside the sponsored projects office.

Start-ups

In a research context, a start-up company is one that is established to develop a commercial opportunity that draws on research assets developed in a university research program. In conventional technology transfer, such start-ups take a license to patents covering research inventions as their primary intellectual property assets. In practice, however, such start-ups are only a small portion of the new venture activity around a university research center. Start-ups may also develop new technologies related to university research findings, share common research instrumentation or data, and benefit from access to the technical and scientific expertise of university personnel. In addition to "technology-based" start-ups, new ventures may also provide services such as design, simulation, or technical support without taking a license to patent rights, or without seeking to develop research technology into commercial products.

Start-ups form a primary element in technology-based economic development strategies, are a primary metric of entrepreneurship programs and business plan competitions, and form the target market for business parks, incubators, and angel investment networks.

Technology transfer

Technology transfer involves the movement of technology—that is practical capability—from an area of expertise to a new area of practice. Conventionally, technology transfer comes in three forms. The first involves movement of technology from a developed nation to a developing country. The second involves the movement of technology established in one industry to uses in other industries. The third involves the movement of research findings into commercial settings. This third form of technology transfer is often what is meant in the context of university research management.

The conventional form of university "technology transfer" involves the identification of inventions, market assessment as to commercial potential, filing of patent applications on the inventions deemed valuable, and a marketing effort to find industry partners willing to undertake the development of commercial products based on the patent rights. This form of technology transfer is reasonable insofar as it goes, but often fails to take into account the many varieties of research assets, the range of ways in which new findings are used in different industries, and the role patents play in these industries. In some industries, such as biotech, patents are a necessary part of business operations, but in others, such as information technology, patents are often seen as an impediment to new technology adoption. If a technology transfer organization fails to identify commercialization partners for its technology, it may keep patents on the books for a number of years, waiting to see whether an industry adopts products that fall within reserved university patent rights. The organization then may seek to assert patent rights against a number of companies, seeking royalty payments. Although such assertive activity is a legal and well-established means of generating monetary value from patent positions, it is not really a form of technology transfer, as there is simply no technology transferred in a patent assert transaction.

University-industry agreements

Universities and companies have many points of engagement. Companies may serve as vendors and suppliers of equipment and services to university researchers and facilities. Companies hire university graduates as employees and faculty members as consultants. In addition, companies may participate in research through sponsored programs, joint research collaborations, donations of cash and equipment, and may serve as advocates for university support through fund-raising and political debates regarding support for higher education.

Research agreements between universities and industry take a range of forms: sponsored research, material transfer agreements, nondisclosure or teaming agreements, publication and distribution agreements, licensing arrangements, services contracts, sales agreements, various forms of stock subscription agreements, affiliates programs and other memberships, and consortium agreements. As these agreements move outside of sponsored projects and conventional patent licensing operations, universities have relatively few resources to address their management. Similarly, as agreements move from procurement of research services and other standard industry agreements, companies generally have neither the time nor interest to deal with custom drafting and the attendant legal review necessary to create new contracting instruments.

Typical sources of disagreement include control of research and publication; allocation of risk in the conduct of research and in the management of results; control of research data and results, including intellectual property; and sharing of commercial upside arising from university research contributions. Other sources of disagreement may include how a contract may be terminated; the effects of such termination on student employees involved and on rights to preliminary research results; governing law and venue; forms of alternative dispute resolution; penalties for failure to meet milestones or produce desired results; nondisparagement clauses or payment for favorable mention; and the handling of F&A rates.

One of the major challenges for the research community is developing new ways in which universities and companies may collaborate in the development of advanced research initiatives and exploit the findings.

RESOURCES

APAX Partners

www.apax.co.uk/APAX_TECH_TRANSFER.pdf

This pamphlet summarizes structured mechanisms for transforming university inventions into commercial products and services. It emphasizes the best practices in technology transfer in five countries: France, Germany, Israel, the United Kingdom, and the United States.

Council on Government Relations (COGR)

www.cogr.edu/

This is an association of research universities located in Washington, D.C. The council supports the development of financial and administrative aspects of federally funded research and provides information for understanding academic operations and the impact of proposed federal regulations on colleges and universities. COGR helps to develop policies and practices of interest to federal agencies and universities involved in research and graduate education.

The Association of University Technology Managers (AUTM)

www.autm.net/

This association consists of thirty-five hundred technology transfer professionals working in academic, research, government, legal, and commercial settings. AUTM promotes and supports technology transfer through education, advocacy, networking, and communication.

CONNECT

www.connect.org/

CONNECT is a public benefits organization fostering entrepreneurship in the San Diego region by catalyzing, accelerating, and supporting the growth of the most promising technology and life science businesses. It is entirely self-supporting through membership dues, course fees, and corporate underwriting for specific programs.

Association of University Research Parks (AURP)

www.aurp.net/

The mission of AURP is to promote the development and operation of research parks that foster innovation, commercialization, and economic competitiveness in a global economy through collaboration among universities, industry, and government.

International Association of Science Parks (IASP)

www.iasp.ws/publico/intro.jsp

IASP is a worldwide network promoting science parks, organizations managed by specialized professionals, whose main aim is to increase the wealth of its community by promoting the culture of innovation and the competitiveness of its associated businesses and knowledge-based institutions.

BIBLIOGRAPHY

Agres, Ted. "I'll See You in Court." *The Scientist*, 2005, *19*(12), 39–41.

Audretsch, David. *Entrepreneurship, Innovation and Economic Growth*. Cheltenham, UK: Edward Elgar, 2006.

Devol, Ross, and Armen Bedroussian. *Mind to Market: A Global Analysis of University Biotechnology Transfer and Commercialization*. Santa Monica, CA: The Milken Institute, 2006.

Hargadon, Andrew. *How Breakthroughs Happen: The Surprising Truth about How Companies Innovate*. Boston: Harvard Business School, 2003.

Kao, John. *Innovation Nation: How America Is Losing Its Innovation Edge, Why It Matters, and What We Can Do to Get It Back*. New York: Free Press, 2007.

Porter, Michael E. *Competitive Strategy: Techniques for Analyzing Industries and Competitors*. New York: Free Press, 1998.

Porter, Michael E. *On Competition*. Cambridge, MA: Harvard Business Review, 1996.

Saxenian, AnnaLee. *The New Argonauts: Regional Advantage in a Global Economy.*, Cambridge, MA: Harvard University Press, 2006.

Shane, Scott, *Academic Entrepreneurship: University Spinoffs and Wealth Creation*. Northhampton, MA: Edward Elgar, 2004.

Walshok, Mary L. *Knowledge Without Boundaries: What America's Research Universities Can Do for the Economy, the Workplace, and the Community*. San Francisco: Jossey-Bass, 1995.

Walshok, Mary L., and Carolyn W. B. Lee. "The Partnership Between Entrepreneurial Science and Entrepreneurial Business: A Case Study of the Integrated Development of UCSD and San Diego's High Tech Economy." In R. P. O'Shea and T. J. Allen (eds.), *Building Technology Transfer within Research Universities: An Entrepreneurial Approach*. New York: Cambridge University Press, 2008.

Walshok, Mary L., and Bengt Stymne. "Collaboration in the Innovative Region." In Rami Shani, A. B., S. A. Mohrman, W. H. Pasmore, B. Stymne, and N. Adler (eds.), *Handbook of Collaborative Management Research*. London: Sage, 2007.

Walters, Kenneth D. *Entrepreneurial Management: New Technology and New Market Development*. New York: Ballinger, 1989.

INDEX